To Andrew and Ross

To the Investa Team

Table of Contents

SAVING INVESTA

INTRODUCTION

In September 2007, Morgan Stanley Real Estate Funds (MSREF) and some of the world's most prominent sovereign wealth and pension fund investors purchased the Investa Property Group, a well-known property company listed on the Australia Stock Exchange, for about $6.5 billion. It was one of the largest "take-private" transactions in the history of Australia.

This transaction was also one of the largest undertaken by Morgan Stanley and its real estate funds group. MSREF was the world's biggest real estate investor with about $185 billion of assets under management at one time and offices worldwide.

To pay for the purchase, MSREF used about $2 billion in equity and $4.5 billion in debt. The heavy reliance on debt funding was typical of private equity firm transactions in the heyday of leveraged investments, and cheap and available debt. However, excessive corporate debt was a primary reason why so many companies failed, and it contributed significantly to the global financial crisis (GFC), that began with Lehman Brothers' bankruptcy in 2008. Such high-risk investment strategies by banks led to stricter U.S. federal legislation and worldwide banking regulatory changes.

The Investa business plan called for a quick sale of Investa assets at peak prices and use of the proceeds to pay down the high level of debt to a more sustainable level. All of the debt was relatively short term (two to five years maturity), it was cross-collateralized (default on one loan, and all loans were due and payable immediately), and it was partially guaranteed by MSREF.

The plan employed a strategy of selling assets quickly after the acquisition at high prices typical of market expectations. Such a strategy can be very rewarding when markets are in balance and values are increasing; but the same strategies are vulnerable to financial market declines. When the GFC commenced within a year of the acquisition, global capital markets froze, and it was impossible to sell hard assets (e.g., office buildings). Investa suffered from high levels of required interest payments that far exceeded income from the property portfolio.

The GFC also stressed Morgan Stanley and its funds business. MSREF suffered losses throughout the world as property values and income declined and commercial buildings competed for a diminishing supply of tenants. While MSREF had guaranteed a substantial portion of Investa's loans, in the depths of the GFC there were no longer sufficient funds to pay the guarantees if Investa defaulted. The bank was also under severe financial pressure and only late support from a Japanese bank saved Morgan Stanley. A default by Investa on $4.5 billion of debt and the loss of $2 billion of equity could have had far-reaching consequences for institutional investors and banks generally. It would further pressure real estate values and commercial markets.

To complicate matters further, Australia has corporate laws that are very punitive toward debtors who do not repay their loans. The country does not have a U.S. Chapter 11-type law that allows corporate reorganization. When a company cannot pay its bills or loans, the normal course is to call in an administrator to take control of the company and liquidate the assets.

When board members believe the company will be unable to pay its bills during the upcoming 12 months, that board must declare the company "insolvent" and cease doing business under Australian law. Failure to do so can result in board directors' personal liability for any debts incurred. Intentional borrowing when a company should have been declared insolvent is also a criminal offense punishable by jail. As chairman of the board and CEO, I was doubly in jeopardy if the company failed and it was determined the company should have been declared insolvent at an earlier date.

With billions of dollars of debt maturing and no obvious source of funds to pay off the debt, insolvency concerns constantly loomed in the background as we tried to navigate through the GFC. I frequently met with outside corporate counsel regarding insolvency laws and their applicability to Investa's circumstances. I was often told that we were operating in a grey area where a reasonable person would have to believe that the company would figure out a way to pay its debts. This vague answer gave me little comfort; many of my senior colleagues transferred their assets into a spouse's name because of solvency concerns.

This story is how Investa managed to survive against all reasonable odds and expectations. It is a perilous journey undertaken in the worst of times.

It is also a personal journey. For the past 25 years, I have been a "corporate fix-it" or "corporate turnaround" guy for property companies. When a company is underperforming or a particular commercial building is at risk, I am a guy that investors can call to remedy the situation.

None of my many professional experiences came close to the demands and difficulties we confronted at Investa during the GFC. None tested a management team as my colleagues and I were tested from 2008 through 2012. As backdrop to the stress and intensity of the Investa experience, I have also shared my life story of growing up near Chicago, my early days working on the factory floor in Cicero, Illinois, and my personal growth and development. It is a story of upward mobility and accomplishment from washing dishes and sweeping streets to the corner CEO office, and from near poverty to substantial wealth. It is also a story of life outside the business world, and the many experiences that characterize and contribute to who someone is.

My life has encompassed the joys and sorrows from one's journey: the happy days filled with sunshine and hope, and the dark days of overcast and depression. I have benefited from years of marital bliss and mutual dependence, and suffered the tears of rejection from a late-in-life divorce. I have experienced poverty and wealth; viewed life from the factory assembly line and the executive corner office; experienced the highs of long-distance running and the lows of the stroke unit in a foreign hospital; and traveled the world conducting business in different cultures and settings.

This is my story. The observations and opinions expressed are mine alone and do not represent any of the companies I have worked for or been associated with, including Investa and Morgan Stanley.

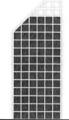

Chapter 1

THE BEGINNING

We were sitting in the executive conference room on the 37th floor of Morgan Stanley's landmark blue headquarters building on Broadway and 48th Street, adjacent to Times Square; the wall of windows overlooked the Manhattan skyline, which sparkled in the late spring sunshine in 2008. Thousands of New Yorkers and visitors scurried about in the streets below; no one inside room 37B noticed.

The conference room was designed to accommodate a bigger audience. The blank video screens supported by an army of high-tech connections and microphones stared at the four people sitting around the oversized table designed to accommodate many more. We all knew each other from previous assignments, and there was an aura of trust, comfort, and mutual respect.

The initial friendly banter masked the fear, which no one mentioned. We were there to discuss Morgan Stanley Real Estate Funds' (otherwise known as MSREF) $6.5 billion investment in Investa Property Group, one of Australia's largest commercial real estate companies. Investa was showing signs of severe financial distress.

The meeting was held amid the backdrop of an emerging financial crisis. Bear Stearns, the venerable Wall Street investment house, had failed and been taken over by J.P. Morgan. The United Kingdom government had seized Northern Rock bank; the Federal Deposit Insurance Corporation (FDIC) was closing failed regional banks in the U.S.

Global property markets were freezing up as the economic world held its breath, fearful of the future.

Jay Mantz, 45-year-old CEO of MSREF, stopped by between meetings. Dressed in a crisp blue dress shirt and contrasting red tie with dark suit pants, Jay fit the image of a frenetic but outwardly calm investment banker and global executive. He rarely stopped moving or asking questions. I suspected Jay's demeanor and quest to know every detail about everything only stopped when he slept. Jay's still relatively youthful look was accented by graying hair, hinting at the stresses and challenges of doing business in what would soon become known as the global financial crisis (GFC).

"Scott, how are you? Are you living in San Diego?" Normally Jay would sit and chat for a few minutes, resuming prior conversations, but today he was rushed and preoccupied. Without waiting for more than a cursory response, he continued, "Thank you so much for considering this assignment. This investment is the largest single investment we have ever made. We cannot afford to lose it."

Jay departed as quickly as he arrived, bound for another meeting for which he was probably late. The life of a division CEO within an investment bank in the spring of 2008 was pressure filled, with little time to rest and reflect. And it would only get worse.

A moment passed waiting for someone to speak.

Chris Niehaus, vice chairman of MSREF and long-term Morgan Stanley principal, began the conversation. Chris was in his 50s and had survived more than 20 years of investment banking. His gently chiseled features suggested someone who was extremely handsome in his youth and was aging gracefully. He spoke in a low but firm tone, suggesting wisdom and experience while commanding attention.

When Chris spoke, people listened. He was relentlessly logical, summarizing facts and conditions, and posing options and alternatives. He rarely threatened or criticized, preferring the clarity of thinking to inspire those around him. Chris caused others to elevate their conversations.

"We have over six billion dollars of equity and debt invested in this company. The company has been underperforming from the day we bought it last September. The local Morgan Stanley office in Sydney is pretty defensive and does not want to admit we have problems. We need someone who knows how to operate a company to go there and help straighten things out. If we fail, it could be catastrophic."

Morgan Stanley had the largest global real estate investment business in the world. It had approximately $185 billion in property investments globally. MSREF had staff and offices throughout the world in major markets and invested money on behalf of pension funds, sovereign-wealth funds, and high-wealth individuals. Like most "opportunistic" private equity funds, MSREF used high levels of debt to fund acquisitions. Investa was the largest single investment MSREF had ever made and was loaded with billions of dollars of debt and fund guarantees. The ramifications of failure would extend to Morgan Stanley and the viability of its huge funds business. It could adversely impact participating banks in Australia, Asia, and Europe, and potentially put further pressure on key credit markets at a time when credit liquidity was increasingly scarce.

Sonny Kalsi was chief investment officer of MSREF and primarily responsible for investing MSREF's billions of dollars in real estate globally. He had an impressive stature; about 6'3" and solidly built. He was an American born of Indian parents and gave the impression of being a really smart guy. His presence seemed to fill a room, both due to his stature and outgoing personality. I always thought if Sonny had not worked at Morgan Stanley, he could have been the founder of a big high-tech company in San Jose with a save-the-world product.

Sonny was also a "deal" guy. He liked to do deals and not talk about issues. He was in the room to get something done; this was not a casual or theoretical conversation. The time to act was now. We both knew this was a negotiation.

"So Scott, will you help us? If you just go down there for six months, you can help get the CEO on the right track."

I looked at Sonny. "Sonny," I said. "The company has too much debt. God himself could not turn this company around without some new equity capital. How much are you willing to put in?"

"We are pretty strapped right now," Sonny replied. "The world economic conditions are not going well, and the fund is closed to new investors; it's hard to raise fresh capital. We are dealing with problems everywhere."

I looked at John Kessler, chief financial officer of MSREF. John was a quiet guy, the type who knew all the answers but was reticent to disclose any. He was smart and articulate, but deferred to Chris and Sonny.

"John," I said, "you always have some money stashed away for a rainy day. It looks to me like it's raining pretty hard. In fact, we are looking at a big-time flood. How much have you squirreled away?"

John is an honest guy. He could not lie, but he did not want to give up his precious reserve. He was worried about the future of all the MSREF investments, not just Investa. He needed as much capital in reserve as possible so he could deal with increasing demands coming daily from Morgan Stanley investment managers seeking to meet financial commitments in Germany, Mexico, the Netherlands, and many other countries around the world. He looked at Sonny, almost pleading for Sonny to respond.

"All right, Scott," said Sonny. "We have $250 million uncommitted. You can have it all but no more. After that, the well is dry, and we are out of business."

I did a quick mental calculation. US $250 million from MSREF coupled with a match from co-investors and exchanged into Aussie dollars meant more than $400 million of fresh capital. It would not guarantee survival but it gave the company a fighting chance.

Sonny spoke with conviction and in definitive terms. I knew him well enough to know he was not holding back. I looked at John; his pained expression told me Sonny had given up the hidden treasure. The time to negotiate was over; it was time to make the deal. After a thoughtful pause, I responded.

"Okay. I'll go for a week and tell you if I think I can help. If we agree, I'll spend up to six months with trips back to the U.S. and trips for my wife to Australia paid by the company. I realize how important this is and will do anything I can to help. Thanks for being open to deploying more equity."

The meeting adjourned quickly, and everyone but Chris Niehaus and I dispersed for other meetings and challenges. Chris and I talked about schedules, and then I took a chauffeured car to the nearby Newark airport for my flight back to California, wondering about faraway Australia and some company in Sydney named Investa, which would test me more than any professional challenge I have faced in the past 40 years.

Chapter 2

LIFE IN THE MIDDLE: BERWYN, ILLINOIS

About 60 years before that meeting in New York, my life started out with a struggle. When Mother discovered she was pregnant with me, her fourth child, her doctor advised her to have an abortion. My mother was a small woman who had three difficult deliveries and several miscarriages. All of her children had weighed over nine pounds at birth, and the doctor feared at her age she would not survive another difficult delivery. She declined an abortion; I am unsure exactly why, but this story would never have happened otherwise.

When I was born at McNeal Memorial Hospital in Berwyn, Illinois, in June of 1947, I weighed over nine pounds and was a "blue" baby. I looked blue from lack of oxygen and was put immediately into a special oxygen-rich compartment.

Berwyn, a close-in suburb of Chicago, was my home as a child. My father's parents moved to Berwyn many years before, and my mother's parents moved there when she was a young woman. Berwyn is not as well-known as its immediate neighbors. To the east is Cicero, Illinois, and the west is Riverside, Illinois. Life in Berwyn was life in the middle between rough-and-tumble Cicero and more-refined Riverside.

Cicero was home to first-generation immigrants, primarily from Eastern Europe. It was a white town, with little tolerance for non-whites. Cicero bordered the west side of Chicago, home to mostly blacks. In the 1950s, Chicago's urban renewal program resulted in the construction of thousands of high-rise public housing units on Chicago's West Side. When black families on the West Side sought a better life in suburban Chicago, Cicero stood in the way.

When Martin Luther King sought to demonstrate racism in the North, he announced his intention to march in Cicero but changed his mind when local police told him it would be "a suicide march." When Al Capone and the Chicago mafia established a Chicago base, they moved into Cicero. Cicero was a town of factories inhabited by immigrants, fighting for a better life. It was a town of hard knocks.

When I was 18 years old and still in high school, I began working in a factory making fiberglass insulation rods during school vacations (more about the factory in a later chapter). Empire Metal Products ("the factory") was located in Cicero. One night, while working at the factory, I was invited to go barhopping in Cicero with one of the younger guys in the factory and his friends. The night was spent in ritual, macho confrontations with other tough guys, demonstrating a willingness to fight for pride and reputation.

In the typical scene, we would walk into a pub or others would enter where we were already established. At first, both groups would ignore each other. Then someone would say something negative – "What do you think you are doing here?" or bump into someone from the other group, causing a confrontation. Like male peacocks preening and exploding their colorful tails in full demonstration, each group would stand tall and appear aggressive, but not so aggressive that the other guys were forced to fight. This was what guys in Cicero did.

Berwyn was home to working families, many second- and third-generation immigrants who moved to Berwyn from Cicero. No one who was wealthy lived in Berwyn; everyone worked in the offices and factories nearby.

In Berwyn, modest single-family homes fronted tree-lined streets. Each home had a grass lawn in front that was carefully maintained and trimmed, and used by the many children and dogs as neighborhood playgrounds. Splashes of seasonal flowers often decorated planter areas between the grass and the houses. The homes were not expensive, but neighbors took pride in the appearance of houses and the yards.

As a child, my favorite activities were baseball, cowboys and Indians, and kick the can. Baseball was a summer pastime. We did not have Little League or baseball fields with organized teams. We played in the streets. All you needed to play was a ball, a bat, and a piece of chalk to mark bases.

Chicago may be the only place in the world where everyone plays baseball with 16-inch balls. These oversized softballs were what we played with, as did everyone else in town. You needed a glove to be a real ballplayer, but you did not need a glove to catch a Chicago softball. If someone could not afford a glove, it was okay; he could still play.

The chalk was to mark at least home plate and second base. Usually, we designated a parked car as first base and, if necessary, another car as third base. With a Chicago softball, it was possible to leave minor dents, but no one in Berwyn owned nice cars. The cars were parked on the street, so an occasional ding was not a big deal.

Now and then, a visitor would come to Berwyn with a shiny new car and stop to visit a neighbor (probably to show off the new car). I recall one time a man parked in front of a neighbor's house; I think he had a fancy new Ford Crown Victoria, two tones, and lots of chrome. It was a beauty, but we considered it just right for first base. The proud owner emerged from inside and became horrified, and then angry, when he realized his new car was being used as a base by a group of ragamuffins. We were quick to disperse whenever an adult screamed at us, which seemed to be pretty often. It was not good to be caught by an adult when we were doing something objectionable in Berwyn.

I recall vividly when our family purchased our first television. It was quite an event when the TV was delivered. Mother did not let us watch much, but we all looked forward once a week to *Gunsmoke* and *Have Gun – Will Travel*. These Western shows and the Saturday morning fare of *The Roy Rogers Show, The Lone Ranger*, and *The Cisco Kid* were the dominant shows of the times.

Like other young boys, my best friend, Bert Hicks (aka Buzzy) and I fought off fierce Indians every summer. We did not have a horse, but we had our trusty companion, my dog Mandy, who barked excitedly whenever we came under attack from hordes of imagined savages.

On summer nights, kick the can was a preferred activity. Behind the houses in Berwyn were alleys. Occasionally, we encountered rats at night, but Mandy and the other dogs in the neighborhood were proficient at killing rodents so the alleys were fairly safe.

In kick the can, one person is "it" and has to find others who are hiding. I never did that well at this endeavor, because Mandy always stayed with me and barked at me if I tried to hide. It was pretty easy to find me; just look for Mandy or listen for her bark.

Mandy was my constant companion. She was a medium-sized shaggy black-and-white terrier mixed breed full of energy and love. She was my sister Margot's dog first, but when I was born, Mandy seemed to take responsibility for me. My mother told me when I was a toddler, she could leave me alone in the backyard even though it was not fenced in. Mandy would watch me, and bark and growl if I tried to leave or if a stranger approached.

One oddity about Mandy was she lifted her leg to pee just like a male dog. Mother told me Mandy played with a male dog when she was a small puppy and must have copied him.

I lived with my parents, my sisters Judy and Margot, and my brother Bing. All of my siblings were much older than me, and we were not close because of the age differences. We lived in a house on the corner of Wisconsin Avenue and 32nd Street. Like other neighborhood houses, it had a big front porch from which adults could look up and down the street and see what was happening. Whenever Mother was looking for me, all she had to do was look up and down the street for Mandy, who was always patiently waiting outside any house I went in.

Mandy would sometimes follow me to school. She would cut across lawns and stay behind bushes to avoid being seen and scolded. Once at school, she would wait outside by the playground for me. Often, the boys played baseball at recess, and Mandy usually joined in chasing the batted balls, often expertly fielding them but always failing to deliver the ball to first base. Mother often complained about being called by the school principal and being asked to come and collect Mandy, whose baseball skills were not appreciated by others.

We did not have school buses in Berwyn. Everyone walked to school or rode bikes. It was safer to walk; bicycles were often stolen. No one took a shortcut through the alleys; big kids would wait for smaller kids to steal their lunches or lunch money. In Berwyn, you were always on guard, even as a little kid.

There was a movie, years ago, entitled *My Bodyguard* with Matt Dillon. It was filmed in Chicago (appropriately, in my view). In the movie, a school kid had a big bruiser of a friend who protected him from others. As a youngster, I had my own version of *My Bodyguard*. For some reason, I befriended John Kilborne, who was one tough guy even in third grade. John was always in trouble with the school. Once he brought garter snakes to school for show-and-tell and then let them go.

John and I were buddies; if you messed with me, you messed with John. I guess it would work the other way, too, but no one was afraid of me coming to John's rescue; they were afraid of John. In third or fourth grade, a gang of boys attacked me and a couple of friends on the playground. John immediately joined the battle, and we prevailed largely due to John's intervention. I recall having to stand up in class, apologize, and renounce fighting on the playground; otherwise, I would have been suspended. It was worth it, however, to cream the other kids who started the fight.

I read in a school reunion flyer years later, that John Kilborne died as a young man. I have no idea if he died in Vietnam or in some street altercation. I know he was a good guy, a little rough around the edges, but his heart was in the right place. In my early school years, I benefited greatly from his help and assistance.

There were always fights in Berwyn, but no one was ever hurt much. An occasional bruise occurred, but mostly it was hurt feelings.

Our house seemed really big to me, but when I visited it years later I was surprised how small the rooms were. Everything seemed big to a small boy.

We had four bedrooms; my parents had one, Margot had one, and Judy had one. Bing and I shared a room that was only accessed by going through Margot's or Judy's rooms. Whenever I wanted to irritate one of my sisters, I would cut through their room at an inopportune time – like when they were getting dressed to go out. It was fun to irritate big sisters at times.

The boys' room was in the back of the house and was hot in the summer and cold in the winter. In the heat of the summer, we left the unscreened windows open. One night I started going to bed, turned on the light, and saw what seemed like an enormous bat flying around my room. I slammed the door shut and ran screaming down the stairs.

The family accompanied me back upstairs. Bing had some kind of a racket – badminton or tennis or whatever. I think someone else had a fishing net, but we were all nervous. When we flicked the lights on and saw the bat, we went into immediate action. I think Bing missed the bat and hit Judy, someone was snared with the net, and Mother tried to restore order from chaos. When things finally settled, the bat had disappeared. Mother tried to convince me the bat had flown out the window, but I did not accept what seemed like a convenient theory. Finally, after lights were switched off and on a few times, the bat reappeared, and Bing nailed him and put the stunned little guy in a box outside in the alley. Without his wings open, the bat was actually pretty small, like a problem that always seems bigger when first encountered.

We had one bathroom in the house, which led to frequent fights and arguments, especially when one of my sisters was in the bathroom

and I had to go. The only option to the one bathroom was a freestanding unsheltered toilet in the attic or the toilet in the damp, dark base-
ment. You had to be truly desperate to use either alternative option. It
was easier to pound the main bathroom door and yell insults.

My father was an optometrist and worked in downtown Berwyn,
which was within walking distance of the house. Sometimes I would
walk toward town and meet him on his way home. We would hold
hands, and I would tell him about my day.

My life in Berwyn changed significantly in early 1954 when I was
six years old. My father had suffered for years with a bad heart. In those
days, bypass surgery had not yet been invented, and the available drugs
were limited. I recall a particularly difficult night with Mother helping
him down the stairs. The next morning, the phone rang and Mother
answered it upstairs, where we had a telephone table and chair in the
hallway. She began weeping, and I ran to her, not accustomed to seeing
her cry. She said, "Your father is dead," and we cried together. More
than 60 years later, I still recall the ring of that telephone as though it
were last week.

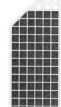

Chapter 3

THE VISIT

A week after the meeting in New York, we arrived in Sydney at 6 a.m. Monday after an overnight flight from Los Angeles, California. After a shower and change of clothes at the Westin Hotel, Chris Niehaus and I met Lynn Thurber for a quick meeting before going to Morgan Stanley's nearby Sydney office. Chris and Lynn are two of the smartest people I have ever met. Chris was a leading banker at Morgan Stanley for over 20 years; he and I have known each other since the 1980s.

Lynn was chairman of LaSalle Investments and was previously its CEO. She was in her 60s like me, had a quick smile, a nice laugh, and a good sense of humor. But once a conversation started, she became serious and was very insightful and perceptive. She was the kind of person it is impossible to fool.

The three of us were the team sent by MSREF to troubleshoot what was wrong with Investa, the big Australian office and land-development company that MSREF bought in late 2007.

At Morgan Stanley's Sydney office, we were ushered into a conference room on the 39th floor of Chifley Tower, with commanding views of Sydney Harbor out to the Heads, where the harbor meets the Pacific Ocean. Australian Navy ships were tied up at Garden Island; colorful green-and-yellow ferries motored about visiting the many wharfs; and sailboats tacked in the fresh breeze. The panoramic view was truly spectacular, but we were there to discuss Investa and could not linger on the amazing sights.

Morgan Stanley has its own waiters, kitchen, and espresso coffee machines, so there would be no shortage of caffeine for us jet-lagged travelers. The three of us drank multiple cups of espresso-style coffee while listening to the local Morgan Stanley team alternately complain about the Investa leadership and claim there were no major problems that could not be resolved with time.

The Morgan Stanley real estate office in Sydney was run by Rei Umekubo, an American of Japanese descent. Sydney was his first assignment running a major office; MSREF was obviously impressed with his work in Japan and his loyalty to the firm, or the company would not have appointed him to run such a remote office. He was clearly a very smart and extremely articulate professional.

Rei was also an enigmatic guy to me. He moved quickly and had a slender build that suggested he was in good physical shape. He had a quick smile and articulated well when he talked, but he kept most things to himself and rarely disclosed information or especially problematic issues. It was as though disclosure of an unsolved issue represented some kind of failure or loss of face. The problems of Investa were buried under paperwork and what had become unachievable budget forecasts and plans. The local office refused to acknowledge what seemed obvious to me – that Investa would not survive following its present course.

Rei was not responsible for making the Investa acquisition decision; he was working in Tokyo at the time. According to Steve Harker, CEO of Morgan Stanley Bank in Australia, everyone involved with the deal had approved moving ahead despite early economic warning signs. They had made a commitment to do the deal and intended to honor that commitment. Subsequently, when conditions deteriorated, some of the employees who left the company claimed they had been unsupportive. When an investment is unsuccessful, everyone blames someone else; when a deal goes well, everyone claims credit. Good deals always have multiple sets of parents; bad deals are orphans. Investa was an orphan deal.

Rei and his staff had hired John Thomas as Investa's CEO after taking control in late 2007. John had never run a big company but had a good track record as chief operating officer at another Australian real estate company. He seemed to enjoy being a big company CEO but struggled with the management burden and high expectations of his Morgan Stanley supervisors.

Chris and I went to see John for lunch after the meeting with Morgan Stanley's local staff the Monday we arrived in Sydney. John came across as a nice guy, with a distinct New Zealand accent and relaxed demeanor. However, we were surprised by the discussion that ensued. First, he complained about the shortcomings of his senior staff. This was a bad sign.

"I need to fire Michael Cook. He is not very good. He spends most of his time staring at his BlackBerry."

"The CFO just is not very good, and we should replace him, too."

John's criticisms of many of his colleagues continued through lunch, although he was complimentary toward a few of his colleagues. He appeared to rely on the acquisition projections that everything would be right in the future.

Rei had told John there would be no more capital available under any conditions and discouraged John from raising the issue. Rei seemed to feel solving the problem without asking for money was a badge of honor, and it was critical to uphold the business plan and underwriting projections despite changing market conditions, which had rendered such forecasts unachievable. In my view, the "Investa bus" was about to drive off the cliff, with its drivers clinging to their defective road map, which was written when economic conditions were more favorable.

Later the same day, Chris Niehaus and I had a tour of Investa's office buildings led by Michael Cook, the same senior executive of whom John was most critical. Cookie, as he was called, was a short guy, a compact bundle of energy, always dressed in a black shirt and colorful tie. He was a nonstop talker, passionate in his beliefs, and fueled by multiple cups of coffee each day. Local coffee shops usually greeted Michael with a smile born of familiarity and the phrase, "The usual?" He also appeared to know everything about the local office market, and seemingly every detail about each building and nearby competitive buildings.

I ascribe to the theory that some people know everything about nothing while others know nothing about everything. Some specialize and some are generalists. Cookie was a specialist; he knew everything about Australian office buildings.

Late that afternoon, I pulled Chris Niehaus aside. "This guy is really impressive. I am thinking that Cookie may be more valuable to this company than the CEO."

Chris replied, "I was thinking the same thing."

That night and each night thereafter, Lynn, Chris, and I met with senior Investa executives, usually without the CEO. Sometimes we split up; Chris could take John or another executive out to dinner while Lynn and I took out a couple of others. We wanted to talk to all the executives individually or in small groups outside the office to understand their views and insights on problems and opportunities.

What emerged was a picture of a company in deep disarray. Many of the executives were waiting for July when their "stay bonuses" were to be paid. Then they intended to leave. No one had sufficient confidence in private equity ownership or senior management to want to stay.

One of the strangest dinners was with a couple of executives, including the head of development. He told us of the many deals he was working on. I asked about the approval process to spend money since I knew the company was hemorrhaging cash and could not survive at its current cash burn rate. He said he had standing authorization to spend $100,000 per project without telling anyone, and he could divide larger projects into multiple smaller ones as necessary to avoid needing an approval.

I suggested new policies were needed to monitor expenditures and approve new projects. In response, the executive threw a temper tantrum and walked out. It was truly a bizarre scene but reflected the silos in which departments operated, and the lack of accountability and financial controls.

Wednesday of that week, the department heads presented their business plans to the three of us and the local Morgan Stanley property team. Each presentation showed a hockey-stick growth profile – no growth now but phenomenal growth coming soon and resulting in a successful accomplishment of the approved business plan. The plans were not credible and clearly not based on market conditions or recent company experience.

Finally, exasperated, I asked one of the department heads, "Did you define the forecasts and results, or were you given the outcomes by senior management and told to put together a presentation showing how you would reach the targets?"

The CEO and the local MS guys were sitting with us and turned to hear the answer. He replied, "We were given the results and told to form a presentation around the required answers."

"Do you believe these results are possible?" I asked.

"No," he replied candidly.

The forecasts reflected wishful thinking and were unrelated to actual business conditions. Hope is never a legitimate business plan. Investa's problems just increased geometrically. There was no realistic possibility of meeting forecasts, and the company was running out of money.

Thursday night, Chris, Lynn, and I sat in the Westin bar after dinner. It was designed to be comfortable with a living-room look featuring sofas and plush chairs in an upscale and overpriced setting. However, none of us was feeling very comfortable. The waitress hovered close by, plying us with salted nuts and snacks in undersized bowls. Chris and I had a beer while Lynn sipped a glass of Australian wine. Chris and

Lynn were flying back to the U.S. the next day; I was scheduled to fly back Saturday.

Chris started the conversation. "The CEO plans to resign tomorrow morning. The question is what happens next. If we leave without a CEO, this place will unravel even faster. Our only hope is for one of us to stay and take on the job. I cannot because of my other MS responsibilities."

Lynn wasted no time in replying that she was chairman of LaSalle and could not take on another job, nor was she willing to move to Australia with family obligations in the U.S.

They both looked at me.

"Hey guys, I am the wrong candidate for this one. I am a shopping-center guy; what do I know about office buildings? And as far as local familiarity, this is my first trip to Australia and I have only been here four days."

Chris responded, "Scott, we need you to do to this. Our real estate platform is under severe pressure; the investors know you and will trust us to fix this if you are involved. We have had a long history together; we really need you."

Morgan Stanley had been good to me through the years, and the company had benefitted from the relationship as well. Much of my family's net wealth came from MS assignments, especially the Center America deal in Houston several years earlier.

"Okay, Chris," I replied. "But I am only committing to six months; you need to find a permanent CEO during this time. And I need to be chairman and CEO; Rei is a nice guy, but I cannot report to someone who is in denial or is defensive about the investment."

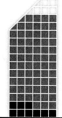

Chapter 4

RIVERSIDE:
THE HOLY GRAIL MEETS
THE GRIM REAPER

My move to Sydney in 2008 was the latest of many moves in my life, beginning when I was a boy. The first move was when my family moved from Berwyn to Riverside; I was 10 years old. The move followed a typical migration pattern just west of Chicago. A frequent goal of people on Chicago's West Side was to move to Cicero, which caused big confrontations because the people from the West Side were black, and the people in Cicero were white. A common goal of Cicero residents was to move to Berwyn. Often, first-generation immigrants lived in Cicero and second- or third-generation residents lived in Berwyn.

Berwyn residents often sought to move to Riverside, which was more upscale. Winding streets, parks, baseball fields, and a more professional group of residents were what Riverside offered. It was located just across Harlem Avenue from Berwyn, but Harlem Avenue was as wide as the Pacific Ocean.

One of my earliest memories was hearing Mother talk about moving to Riverside. Prior to my father's death, my parents actually put a lot in Riverside under contract to purchase. They planned to build a house. When my father died, there were no longer sufficient funds or income to buy or build a house, and it was a significant setback for Mother's dream of moving the family to Riverside.

When I was in fourth grade, Mother finally succeeded in buying a house in Riverside. By then Margot was in high school (in Riverside, of course), and Judy and Bing were out of the house. Our Riverside home was a modest, brick house, adjacent to the Lutheran church and across the street from the elementary school. It was often mistaken for being part of the church and eventually Mother sold it to the church and moved into a small duplex home in North Riverside.

Riverside was, and still is, a nice, middle-class suburb of Chicago. Frederick Law Olmstead, who planned Central Park in New York City and was a well-known city planner and architect, planned the town. It had virtually no straight streets, which caused non-residents to inevitably become lost when visiting. Gas lamps gave character but provided minimal street lighting at night until they were subsequently replaced by electric streetlights.

The kids in Riverside were into playing baseball and football and not into fighting. There were organized Little Leagues with real bases. There were parks scattered throughout the community, which provided opportunities for pick-up football games in the fall and baseball in the summer.

Soon after I moved to Riverside, some of my friends from Berwyn rode their bikes over to see me. I was at a new friend's house in Riverside, and when the Berwyn crowd arrived, they were not impressed with the Riverside "wimps." I remember yelling at my recent friends not to beat up my new friends and to leave us alone. That moment was the end of old friendships and the beginning of new ones. Life was so different across Harlem Avenue.

Living across the street from the elementary school had pluses and minuses. I didn't need much time to get to school, and we often played baseball on the concrete playground during the weekends, which was very convenient. However, I recall skipping school one day to watch a late season Yankees – White Sox baseball game on TV and was shocked when the principal knocked on the door to find out why I was not in school. She knew Mother worked and wanted to make sure I was okay (but not completely okay). That was the last time I skipped school in Riverside.

We moved to Riverside in 1957, about three years after my father died. My mother's parents came up from Arkansas to help out. Mother was working full time then at a bank in Chicago.

I remember Granddaddy Corson as a kind man with a shock of white hair. He was often reading a book in his favorite chair when I came home from school. He always showed keen interest in how my day had been and what I had learned. He was never able to attend a university but did take mail-order courses, which were an early predecessor to Internet learning, and earned an accounting degree. He was a telegraph operator like his father but changed careers when his chosen profession became obsolete.

Granny Corson was an active woman. She was always puttering around, sometimes nagging Granddaddy, making meals beginning with breakfasts, and keeping current with events. She introduced me to pancakes; she insisted I started the day with a good breakfast. She was an active member of the Women's Christian Temperance Union that supported anti-liquor laws.

Shortly after Granddaddy and Granny returned to their home in Hamburg, Arkansas, Granddaddy died. Within three years, I had lost my father and my grandfather. It was a sad time, especially for my mother, who had lost her only sister, her husband, and her father in fairly rapid succession.

Later the same year, Mom's only brother, Uncle Barney, moved in with us. He had been the manager of a radio station in Shenandoah, Iowa, and his family still lived there. His specialty was country and western (C&W) music. When WLS, a big Chicago radio station, decided to convert to a C&W format, they hired Uncle Barney as its new station manager. He moved in with us until he could bring his family to Chicago.

I think Uncle Barney lived with us for about six months – it was less than a year – but he became the man in the family. My mother told of how Barney was able to take her mind off her troubles and how she would go with him to C&W dances sponsored by the radio station. I remember Uncle Barney as a friendly man with a preference for brightly colored (e.g., Hawaiian) shirts. He also chain-smoked cigarettes.

Shortly after he moved his family to nearby Evanston, we were having a small birthday party for my mother. The phone rang and it was Natalie, Barney's oldest daughter. I remember Mother taking the call and protesting loudly almost frantically, "That can't be." Uncle Barney died suddenly of walking pneumonia, less than a year after Granddaddy died.

There was just too much loss in such a short time. Every man I was close to had died in a short period of time; the loss was even greater for my mother. I withdrew, and Mother began to rely on a couple of stiff drinks every night after work.

When I turned 12 years old, I entered sixth grade at Hauser Junior High School, which was about a mile from home. In good weather, I rode my bike to school (unlike Berwyn, bikes were not usually stolen from the school lot). In the winter, it was a long, cold walk. I think the harsh winter weather toughened everyone a bit and probably led to fewer complaints about non-weather things.

At Hauser Junior High School, I was the dishwasher. Always broke, I got the job washing dishes in the school cafeteria. For my efforts, I received free meals (and possibly minimal wages; I do not recall). I don't know if there were government subsidized lunch programs then, but even if there were, my Mother would not have let any member of the family accept government assistance (like free meals). If you needed money, you worked for it. Since I needed money, I worked. It was a pretty simple concept. I never received an allowance.

I also tried delivering newspapers for a while. In those days, kids on bikes delivered newspapers. There were two things I did not like about delivering papers. First, waking up and starting work before dawn. Second, while I became proficient throwing the *Chicago Tribune* and *Chicago Sun-Times* from my bike, I never could throw the skimpy *Hlasatal* Czech newspaper proficiently. It was too thin, and the wind would take the paper off course. If the newspapers were not on the steps or porch, subscribers would complain. Too often I had to fish the Czech paper out of bushes, which delayed progress and usually woke up the dogs, thereby angering the adults and making my life miserable. My newspaper days lasted one season.

During the summer holidays, I had a lawn service business. If I cut and trimmed our lawn, I had use of the lawnmower to cut others' yards and earn money each summer. I did this until I was old enough to obtain a legitimate work permit (my sophomore year in high school).

I attended Riverside Brookfield (RB) High School. Their official nickname was the Bulldogs; the unofficial name was "the Zoo." Our school was adjacent to the Brookfield Zoo, and non-RB students often called us the Zoo, as if non-human animals attended RB. It was an unfair accusation. Most of us were pretty normal.

RB had a wide range of students from a broad array of families. It was a regional school, drawing from Riverside and several less upscale communities. It was similar to Memorial High School in Houston, where my sons, Andrew and Ross, attended, but with more boys and girls thinking of vocational training and fewer focused on college. Girls were required to take home economics courses and boys were required to take Industrial Arts or "shop," which included semesters on woodworking, print setting, auto repair, and electricity.

I was expected to play football at RB because my brother had been captain of the football team when he was there. I played center on the freshman team, and I hated it. The coaches were very tough, and I did not respond that well to being yelled at and slapped around. They seemed to yell a lot and teach very little. I do not think our team won any games that year. When my freshmen coaches were promoted to the sophomore team my second year, I decided not to play. My football career was over; Mother was not pleased with my decision not to play football and, for many years thereafter, was very critical of me for quitting.

I also played on the golf team as a freshman in high school, although I was not one of the better players. For my sophomore year, I
decided to play recreational tennis instead of golf. Today, as I look back,
I think my decision to drop golf may have been in part a rejection of
what my mother wanted me to do. She was an avid golfer, and I did not
want to be like her. It sounds very juvenile, but that is the age I was.

My relationship with my mother was not very good during my
teens. She was a short woman with red hair and a steely determination.
She raised a family, worked at a big Chicago bank, Northern Trust,
rising to become only the second woman vice president in the bank's
history. "Indomitable" may be a good descriptive term for Mother from
my point of view.

However, her drinking became a significant problem following
the deaths of so many family members; she did not hold her liquor well
and she often became abusive at night. Unfortunately, I was the only
one home at the time.

The tirades usually included unfavorable critiques of me for not
playing football (or golf) my second year: "You are a quitter and quitters
never amount to anything."

The soliloquies often incorporated her Southern-bred extreme political views about racial segregation and her struggles at work in a male-
dominated banking system.

At first I argued with her, which resulted in escalation and confrontation. Then I just ate in silence and tried to ignore Mother's ram-
blings. During my teenage years, I ate virtually every dinner in silence.
Throughout my years in Riverside, I never brought a friend to our house.
I was too embarrassed by Mother's drinking and intoxicated behavior.

One outlet I had during this dark time was my oldest sister, Judy,
who was 12 years older than me. She had married after graduating from
Miami University in Ohio, where she had been the newspaper editor,
and lived nearby. When things seemed too bad to continue, I could
walk to Judy's and talk to her or her husband, Bob, or just hang out

away from Mother. Judy had red hair, like my mother, but was more relaxed and was always welcoming and willing to listen. She had a social personality that attracted everyone, but she was a bit unforgiving if I ever used incorrect grammar. She taught English at nearby Morton High School. If Judy had not lived close by and been there for me, I do not think I would have survived my feelings of isolation and depression.

I had two good friends in high school and several others to hang around with. My best friends were Joe Dvorak and Jim Segin. Jim's parents were older and didn't seem to like having us around, so we typically hung out at Joey's when we needed a place to land. Joey was an only child, and his mom and dad were wonderful people, who always took an interest in our comings and goings and treated us like young adults. Whenever we were there late at night, Joey's mom always had a spread of food and sodas for us.

When I was in college, Joey asked me to be his best man in his wedding. He was getting married in Missouri when I was still in school. Frankly, I did not have the money to get there, much less rent a tux and pay for a place to stay. I was too embarrassed to tell him I could not afford to come, so I made up another excuse. I still feel badly to this day for not finding a way to go.

In high school, I loved government and economics classes and disliked math and science. When I was a junior, I worked as Riverside campaign chairman for a state senator who was running for reelection. His opponent was from Riverside, and he could not get an adult to work on his campaign in Riverside, so I was given the opportunity. Mostly, my friends and I delivered campaign literature door-to-door, because no one had money to advertise. We were able to contact most of the houses in Riverside, and as a result, my candidate ran fairly well in Riverside and won his town of LaGrange, ensuring his reelection. I also worked as a poll watcher and called in election-night results to the party headquarters and local media. That was really my first taste of politics, and it was a heady experience to influence the outcome of a political contest and influence, in a small way, the course of future government policy.

When asked what we wanted to be when we grew up as part of an in-class survey, I considered responding, "president of the United States," but I thought this may be a bit overreaching, so I put down "United States senator." I had no interest in business or anything related.

As a junior, I started a new club at high school to discuss current events. We called it "The Forum." The club lasted two years, had few members, and ceased when my friends and I graduated. There was not much interest in public affairs and government in high school, but that was typical of the times.

I have always felt a need to help others less fortunate. I am unsure where this need came from, but it has been part of my life from early days. In high school, it manifested by helping tutor "ghetto kids" in Chicago. On Saturday mornings when I was a senior in high school, I drove to Marillac House, a Catholic church-sponsored outreach program for poor and minority children on Chicago's West Side. There, I tutored young boys in math and reading, but their interest level was limited. They were there because their mothers sent them, or they wanted the free snacks that were available. They also wanted to play basketball in the indoor gym, especially in the winter when it was not possible to play ball on the outdoor playgrounds. It did not take me long to realize how to connect with these kids. If they paid attention and worked with me on their assignments, I would take them upstairs and play basketball with them for the second half of the morning. Basketball played a very large role in the aspirations of black youth then and continues to serve as a major motivation for minority boys in poor neighborhoods. I was surprised how important it was to the lives of these children.

I really did not care for the years I spent in high school. Troubles at home overshadowed opportunities at school. I dated girls and went to dances, but never had a steady girlfriend. I graduated in June 1965, with honors in government and Bs in everything else.

The difficult times growing up probably helped prepare me for the pressures and challenges of running troubled companies. I believe generally that people who overcome adversity are less fazed when confronted with obstacles and problems later in life. Still, I would have preferred a happier youth.

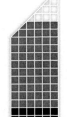

Chapter 5

THE FIRST SIX MONTHS
AT INVESTA

Soon after the night in the Westin bar when I agreed to become
Investa's CEO, the many challenges were becoming more apparent. I
spent considerable time walking the floors of Investa's offices, meeting
staff, talking about their work, and generally conveying assurance and
confidence in Investa's future.

"Hi, I'm Scott MacDonald, the new CEO," I said as I shook
hands with another Investa employee.

"Nice to meet you. I am ___. I just started working here, too,"
was a common reply.

I was confused. The company was running out of money but still
hiring new employees at a seemingly rapid pace.

I met with Bonita Croft, the head of Human Resources (HR)
for Investa and a wily veteran, who had held senior positions at other
firms, including Brambles, before coming to Investa. Bonita was very
smart and knowledgeable about the ways of Australian companies,
people, and, specifically, Investa. I often relied on her advice.

"Bonita, I seem to be meeting lots of people who just started work
here. Have we been hiring lots of new employees lately?"

"We don't know exactly," she replied. "Each department hires
their staff. Often they put the new staff on contract and don't notify
HR. We don't know precisely how many employees we have, including

contractors, or how many recent hires."

"Bonita, this is nuts," I replied in amazement. "You need to know and approve every employee hiring."

"I agree," she said, "but the department heads have insisted on the freedom to operate their business units without HR oversight, and the previous CEO went along with this. It makes no sense; but that is how it has been done here."

"Bonita," I asked, "please send out a memorandum indicating there is now a hiring freeze, and no department is authorized to add any staff without filling out the HR paperwork and obtaining my signature. This includes contract employees. No one gets hired unless you and I think they are essential and fully justified."

"This will be interesting," she replied with a smile I had not seen from her before.

We had about 680 employees at the time – we were unsure exactly how many. In recent months, we were adding employees at the same time our cash flow was running about $10 million a month negative. No one was connecting the dots: not the company executives, not the department heads, not Morgan Stanley's asset managers. I began to look at the various departments.

"So what is Project Enterprise? That department seems to have several highly paid employees, and I don't understand its mission."

"It is a department focused on formulating and implementing change management to make us more efficient."

"Okay, so how much money are we spending in order to implement money-saving strategies?"

"A few million dollars a year."

"So if we eliminated the department responsible for finding ways to save money we could save millions?"

"Yes, I guess so."

I eliminated that department soon thereafter, but even the obvious decisions were difficult because they affected people's lives. I knew what had to be done but anguished at the personal consequences of my decisions. For example, I still struggle knowing that one employee who we retrenched was a widow with four young children. She was making a very high salary, about $250,000 a year base salary with a bonus on top. I knew she would likely struggle to replace that income to support her family. However, the company was going broke, and I could not maintain the existing cost structure.

Generally, the department heads were responsible for terminating employees. The day we let people go, I recall seeing Lloyd Jenkins, head of our land development group, as white as a ghost. "Lloyd, you look terrible. Are you okay?"

"No. I just terminated a woman who sat on the floor and wailed. I felt so helpless," he replied. I understood completely.

One department head lost his voice and could not speak when confronted with the task of retrenching a senior attorney. Another colleague had to step in and finalize the termination. It was such a difficult and stressful time, but we had to do it or we would not have survived.

There were so many things wrong with the company and so much to do. I knew I was in a strange place and needed to rely on those around me if we were to survive. I worried that I would be perceived as the "ugly American" CEO who thought he knew everything and ordered people around. To be successful, everyone at Investa needed to buy into the changes and be part of the solution. I could provide leadership, but the solutions had to come from my new colleagues, and we had so little time as the cash continued to diminish.

At the same time that I was struggling to plug the financial dike, my wife of 30 years, who stayed in California, was showing increasing hostility in frequent and highly accusatory emails. Our relationship had deteriorated in recent years, and I naïvely thought some physical separation would help us. As the emails from home became increasingly negative, I was unsure how to respond; it was not what I had expected. When I tried to correct what I knew to be wrong, that only seemed to escalate the negativity, so I often just declined to respond.

Between the pressures of work, negative reinforcement at home, and living in a strange land with no friends or family, my stress levels escalated. I was not sleeping and not dealing well with the circumstances. As a result the dire consequences to my health were about to become apparent.

At work, we needed to reduce excessive operating costs, but we also needed to increase revenue. The quickest way to increase revenue was to lease vacant space in our office buildings and sell lots in our already developed subdivisions.

I asked the head of our office group, Campbell Hanan, "Why can't we lease this office space? The market seems okay and the building is top-notch."

"We can, but Morgan Stanley will not approve the lease deals. When they bought the company, they placed very high values on the properties, which were based on extremely high rent projections. With current market conditions, we cannot achieve those projections. So the space remains vacant and will likely stay vacant."

"Okay, let me understand. We have a vacant space and a credit tenant who wants to lease the space at market rates, but the Morgan Stanley guys are resistant because they do not want to admit that their underwritten rents are no longer valid?"

"Yes, that is how we see it."

"Lease the space. Now."

"What will you tell Morgan Stanley?"

"I have a meeting with Rei later this week and will explain we need to generate some cash flow quickly. I am sure he will understand."

A few days later, I sat in a small conference room with Rei Umekubo and his key staff on the 39th floor of Chifley Tower. The views over the harbor and out to the Pacific Ocean were still spectacular, but once again I did not have time to savor them. We talked about the many issues confronting Investa, and Rei asked me a question. I started to answer but could not speak. I talked, but no words came out. It was a strange and unfamiliar feeling.

Finally, someone joked that I must be working too hard. When I continued to struggle, Rei asked, "Scott, are you okay?"

"No."

"Should we call for medical help?"

"Yes." I was unable to utter another single syllable word.

The medic arrived soon and not much later I was in an ambulance en route to the St Vincent's Hospital emergency room. I had recovered the ability to talk but felt weak and confused. I had suffered a minor stroke known as a transient ischemic attack or TIA.

The stress and pressure had pushed me over the edge; the remaining issue was whether I would suffer another bigger and potentially disabling stroke or whether this TIA was an isolated incident. After a long day in the emergency room, I felt better and refused to stay in the hospital overnight. I returned to work two days later but was worried, especially in light of my father's death by stroke at age 47. I felt I had to appear engaged and confident to the hundreds of Investa employees who looked for signs and reassurances that everything would be okay.

Soon thereafter, Bonita came into my office and laid out the results from a confidential employee survey undertaken just before I started.

"The good news," she said, "is we had widespread employee participation – over 80 percent of all Investa employees filled out the confidential employee survey on work conditions. The bad news is no one likes to work here. Compared to other companies who undertake similar surveys, Investa is in the bottom 3 percent in employee satisfaction. It is really difficult to be that bad. When asked if they would recommend Investa as a place to work to a friend, the overwhelming answer was no."

Throughout the first year at Investa, I corresponded with the MS-REF executives in New York using my personal email account from my apartment. The outlook was so dire I did not want to risk someone at

Investa seeing the extent of the issues and problems we discussed each week. The emails were sent to the MSREF executives' regular company email addresses; the condition of Investa was well known within Morgan Stanley; our concern was to retain Investa employees who would be essential to execute a corporate turnaround.

We started senior executive meetings at Investa every Friday morning. I needed to break down the silos and begin a culture of communicating. First, we drafted a mission statement. Who was Investa? What did we want to be when we grew up? What were our strategic advantages, and in what areas were we unlikely to achieve a position of market dominance? A mission statement took shape with a focus on office buildings, land development, and funds management. Department heads talked through issues and shared ideas. A dialogue began to reinforce the concept of being one company and likely to survive or perish together.

We also needed better communication with our employees, so I started a CEO call every month. I stood in front of the entire company (branch offices called in), talked about the company honestly and candidly, and answered all questions. Often I asked department heads to report about what their departments were doing and what issues they were dealing with. By communicating opening and honestly, employees felt they understood why the company was undertaking specific actions. They also felt a part of the company by being involved and asking questions or submitting questions or comments confidentially through an electronic suggestion box.

I tend to be a bit more passionate and emotional than my Australian colleagues and do not hesitate to show my feelings at times. On one CEO call, I started talking about the election of President Obama and choked up a bit in recounting how I never dreamed a black man could be president in light of America's very recent history of racism.

The next day I asked Bonita what she thought of her emotional CEO; I thought I had performed badly. She replied it was definitely unusual, but everyone seemed to feel connected to me as I talked. Some evidently teared up and others stared at their shoes and tried to control their own emotions. A few employees stopped by the next day and said how good they felt working for someone who was so open by sharing personal thoughts and feelings, which made me feel better.

Everything was communicated with employees, even confidential matters that are normally not discussed. I was working on a big deal with another company, and its CEO said, "Scott, the only people at our company who know about our discussions are the three people in this room. We are a listed company and cannot afford a premature leak. Can I assume you have kept these discussions completely secret as well?"

Jonathan Callaghan, our corporate counsel, looked at me with a smirk and a barely concealed sense of hidden amusement. Everyone at Investa knew about our negotiations, and no one had leaked the information. I had a mutual trust with the employees but was unsure how to explain this.

"Peter, we have not held the information quite as tightly as you, but we have it under control. I am confident it will not leak out."

In the midst of the economic downturn and between meetings with insolvency attorneys and calls with Morgan Stanley in New York, I asked for plans to expand the employee break room. I wanted employees to have a place to eat lunch, meet in casual circumstances, and have a beer together Friday after work.

We spent $500,000 in the midst of the downturn to create an employee area and foster informal communication and bonding. Most of my senior colleagues thought I was nuts, but in hindsight, the break room was a great success, facilitating employee interaction and building corporate loyalty. I often ate lunch with the employees, and we talked about Investa and the world in general. It served to bond us together as a team, better able to confront the challenges ahead.

It was really difficult to remove the department silos that had developed in the past. I merged residential land development with commercial land development and brought the residential guys from

Clarendon Homes into our office. This merger brought efficiencies and broke down the development department silo. The head of the development division departed and was replaced by a residential guy more committed to teamwork and cooperation.

Our forecasts showed that significant growth in funds management would drive future business profits. We were predicting an increase in FUM (funds under management) from about $1.4 billion to $7.5 billion in four years. Morgan Stanley had hired a full team of experienced fund managers and executives for Investa about the same time that the funds management business began a period of consolidation and decline.

We had two divisions within Funds Management: wholesale or institutional funds, and retail funds. I understood the wholesale funds concept and spent considerable time meeting with institutional investors and supporting our staff's efforts to increase our presence in this business. But I was immediately uncomfortable with the retail business of operating funds for small mom-and-pop investors. At one time, we had 20,000 investors in a few retail funds.

In Australia, the retail funds model, in my view, went something like this. A financial advisor sells an investment in your fund to his or her small clients and keeps a big fee (historically about 4 percent of the investment principal). The fund then needs to distribute a big dividend to meet the investor expectations. To be able to distribute a big dividend, fund managers typically buy high-risk, poor-quality properties, which offer high yields but carry the greatest risk. Even then it is difficult to distribute a sufficient dividend to compensate for the high advisor front-end fee and high fund operating expenses. For those reasons, funds typically distribute more than the income they earn and make up the shortfall by borrowing from banks.

This type of scheme works only as long as property valuations are increasing and banks agree to increase loan amounts on the high-risk portfolio. This was not a good business model and did not survive well

in the GFC. I sold the retail funds business, and we refocused on growing the institutional funds business. Our flagship office fund, ICPF (Investa Commercial Property Fund) increased in investment scale from
less than $1 billion to more than $2 billion in five years under Pete
Menegazzo's leadership and is a major success story.

When I terminated the CFO of Funds Management, the entire
Funds group walked out for the day. They were a tight-knit siloed unit,
and the CFO was popular. I knew we needed better financial reporting and management and weathered the protest. I also knew the group
needed some time to recoup and adjust, and left them alone for a few
days. Still, I was worried their lagging morale would affect the performance we desperately needed. Eventually, I folded the entire funds
management team into the larger office group to take out another silo.
I also eliminated the group executive role for funds management.

Clarendon Homes was spun off into its own company platform
and became an independent company no longer part of Investa. This allowed greater focus on what we did best: own and manage office buildings, and develop land.

A focus on controlling costs did not mean we were not spending
money on productive initiatives. We lacked a marketing department
when I started. One woman coordinated responses to journalists but
resigned to take a more promising job soon after I started. Within the
first six months, we started a formal marketing department and hired
new and transferred staff from other departments. If we were ever going
to maximize near-term revenues and achieve longer-term enterprise and
brand value, we needed to market and promote our land projects as well
as our corporate presence.

We also needed to improve our back-office technology, which was
obsolete and the result of years of under-investment. My first day at
work, Campbell Hanan and I videotaped a message to employees about
the change in CEO and corporate direction. Unfortunately, our computers were so antiquated, most employees could not play the video on

their desktop units.

Another time I was given a DVD with an important presentation on it. I opened my DVD drive and saw only an empty space. Our computers were not equipped to run DVDs. Subsequently, I received a call from our Melbourne office informing me that their printers only printed in Sydney, so employees were taking projects home to print.

I hired an outside technology consulting firm to review our systems; they reported back they had never worked with a company before that had no standard operating procedures, and no standard equipment configuration or policies. Our computers and servers were held together by a series of technical Band-Aids. Whenever something broke down, which was often, the tech guys would develop a temporary fix.

In our first employee survey, the top complaint was that the computers did not work regularly, and system breakdowns were frequent, preventing employees from doing their jobs. I replaced the head of IT, who was a finance manager, with Neal Noble, a topnotch experienced technology manager, and we subsequently spent millions of dollars upgrading systems, people, and procedures. Later surveys showed the employees were happy with their access to technology and had virtually no complaints with their computers or technology.

Over time we simplified the Investa business model. We became a company with two departments: office and land development. Seven divisions with 680 employees became two departments with 240 employees, and the company's results and cash flow began to improve. Future employee surveys showed Investa in the top quartile of all companies surveyed in terms of employee satisfaction. By the end of my first six months, the company was performing much better as a team and with clear direction and focus. Still, we had a crushing amount of debt, which imperiled our survival.

In December 2008, less than six months after I started at Investa and shortly before Christmas, my wife sent me an email indicating she had commenced divorce proceedings to terminate our 30-year marriage, hired a divorce attorney, and filed papers. Her advice was for me to secure my own attorney, and she would see me in court.

I was initially in shock. Our marriage had deteriorated, but I did not think it would end in divorce. She refused my calls, and six months of expensive legal battles ensued. I was so naïve and unprepared. As her attorney made numerous accusations, all of which were completely false, I spent every weekend responding to the charges. I kept asking myself what I did to the woman I lived with for 30 years that turned her into one so hostile and accusatory. Because I could not communicate with her, I could only wonder and search within.

We had two mediation sessions in the U.S. as required by the court, but she was not interested in compromising or finding common ground. She was hostile and sought revenge, but I was never clear on why. I never had an affair or strayed from my marriage vows, but it seemed I was completely responsible in her eyes for her unhappiness.

My doctor and a therapist both told me I was depressed and asked if I wanted medication, but I declined. I had been through difficult times earlier in life and had survived without medication; I knew I would have to navigate once again through the dark days and did not want my survival skills impaired by drugs.

At one point, I had dinner with two friends while in the U.S. I had just finished a mediation session that was more accusation than finding common ground and solutions. Gary Cunningham and Mike Axelrad both looked at me and one said, "Scott, you look terrible."

I responded, "It's just not fair. I have tried to be a good father and husband. I have made a lot of money and freely offered half to Jill, but she wants much more, and we can't even have an amicable discussion."

Gary and Mike laughed. Both had been divorced but had remarried. One said, "Scott, why do you think things should be fair? Once you accept that nothing is fair, you will find a solution and move on." It was good advice.

The divorce was finalized a year after I started at Investa. The emotional scars took much longer to heal. In one sense, my ability to throw myself at all the problems at work during the week probably let me take my mind off of the adversarial divorce proceedings. But the weekends were really difficult and depressing for me. Somehow, I could solve complex corporate problems but found myself completely incapable of understanding, much less solving, the challenge of an unhappy wife, resulting in a failed marriage.

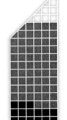

Chapter 6

LESSONS FROM THE FACTORY

The management and leadership skills required to lead Investa were learned from many earlier experiences. I never took a formal management course or seminar, but I have always been viewed as a good and effective manager. Learning to manage and lead others began with observations while working in a factory.

I had worked from the time I could push a lawnmower in grade school. I washed dishes in junior high school and delivered newspapers for a time. When I was a sophomore in high school, I was able to get a work permit and took a job bagging groceries and stocking shelves at the local supermarket (Hillman's Fine Foods). The next summer I worked in a local pharmacy operating the cash register, cleaning, and stocking shelves. The pharmacy job paid $1 per hour.

My family was scraping by, and all of the children were expected to provide their own spending money from an early age. It was no different for me than Bing, Judy, or Margot. We were expected to work and generally take care of our own financial needs.

In high school, I secured a job working at Empire Metal Products in Cicero, Illinois. The starting pay was almost $2 an hour, which was considered good money at the time. I worked at the factory every summer and many vacation times from 1964 until 1971 when I was in graduate school and was required to have a professional internship after my first year. Factory work did not qualify.

The factory was divided into three workspaces including corporate offices, the main factory floor, and a galvanizing pit. The front, low-rise and unassuming brick building was the office, where the "white shirts" worked. The president of the company and the executive vice president, who became president later, frequently came out to the assembly line and knew all the workers by name and skill.

The main factory was an assembly line to manufacture fiberglass insulation rods, which were used to ground utility poles. The concrete floor, stained but swept clean daily, supported big tables of fiberglass rods, large vertical ovens, tanks of chemicals, and a variety of machines needed to create and test the rods. Overhanging doors big enough to allow for small trucks to pass through lined one side of the floor facing the parking lot. Similar doors lined the other side, but were generally closed because they fronted an adjacent railroad track accessing another factory.

The rods were made from liquid fiberglass and chemicals; heavy metal castings were galvanized and attached to each end of the rods using powerful resins, which held the castings in place. The castings were baked in hot ovens, after which the rods were buffed and cleaned, and the completed rods were tested in a stretching machine. The factory was always hot – Chicago summers are hot and humid to begin with – but the ovens made things much worse. There was no air conditioning; we opened overhanging garage doors to try to achieve some minimal level of air circulation, helping to dissipate the aroma of chemicals, which often filled the air. There were signs warning about not breathing in the chemicals, but the signs might just as well have said don't breathe the air.

Years later I visited Kingsport, Tennessee, where the Hahn Company and then Plaza Properties owned a shopping mall. Kingsport is home to the largest chemical plant in the world, and the air smelled like chemicals. When I asked a resident if the odor bothered him, he replied, "It [the air] smells like money." That was how we felt in the factory.

The work was hot and dirty. I wore a white T-shirt and jeans; and by the end of each day the T-shirt was more black than white.

But I felt fortunate to have a good paying job, and I did not mind the working conditions.

My fellow workers were a mixture of immigrants from Eastern Europe (Poles, Hungarians, and Czechs), migrants from Appalachia, an Irishman, and two brothers from the local neighborhood. I learned a lot from this odd mixture of blue-collar workers.

One day I was working on the machines that buffed the fiberglass. It was incredibly repetitious and boring. The guy next to me, Gus, was an older fellow who had emigrated from Eastern Europe. His command of English was not too good, but I realized Gus was a pretty smart person. As I stood working at the buffer, I asked Gus why he did this job day after day. It was okay for me because I knew I would be leaving for something better at the end of each vacation, but for Gus there was no end in sight. Gus looked at me and said in his broken English, "It is not for me, but for my children. It is too late for me, but my kids will have a better life here." I think Gus summed it up for his generation of new Americans.

The most prestigious job on the factory floor was in the shipping department. Sweeney, the Irishman, was in charge of the shipping department. He was the only full-time employee in the shipping department and was responsible for making sure the rods were shipped to the correct destinations, per the orders that flowed to him. His job actually required some thinking. For rush orders, Sweeney would go out to the floor and ask employees to prioritize the processing of some rods over other orders.

Sweeney was really Richard Sweeney, but everyone called him by his last name. He was trim in contrast to many of the workers who showed the effects of after-work beer and starch. He had white hair, which I assumed was premature, a quick smile, and a short laugh that never stopped his work motion. He had a never-ending list of stories, which he could spin day after day without repetition.

Because everyone respected Sweeney, they would accommodate his requests even if it meant working late. If the foreman or one of the corporate types asked the workers to do something that involved more work, there was little cooperation. With this experience, I learned that respect from fellow workers was more important than job titles in getting things done.

Since Sweeney was a department of one and most of the other factory workers could not read English and would be useless in shipping, it was important for Sweeney to never get sick. In fact, he never missed a day of work due to illness. Sweeney told me that when he felt bad, he just worked harder. Sweat was the cure to any fever. Loading and unloading trucks and packing and hauling heavy boxes of fiberglass rods were quick ways to work up a sweat.

One summer we were really busy shipping orders, and I worked most of the summer with Sweeney. I never missed a day of work at the factory either. I needed the money and now I had another reason to drag myself to work even if I felt badly: working was good for curing sickness. Since that summer, I have only missed work two times due to illness in my entire career. In both cases, I developed severe diarrhea when we lived in San Diego and could not leave the safety of a bathroom. My near-perfect attendance for the last 40+ years of working has been the result of a loyalty to my employer for paying me, and Sweeney showing me how I could work through whatever ails me.

Another group of workers at the factory were from Appalachia. The guys from Eastern Europe were here because they wanted to be; the colleagues from Appalachia were here temporarily until they raised sufficient money to move back home. They had a tether to their homes in the hills of Appalachia; if you listen to C&W music, there is a frequent theme of longing to be back home.

I recall during President Johnson's administration, he was determined to fight the "War on Poverty." His advisors believed the chronic poverty in Appalachia was due in part to inadequate infrastructure; so the government embarked on an extensive road-building program to connect Appalachia to the rest of the country. I do not know if the new highways attracted business to Appalachia; however, I do know that they made it easier for the residents to leave, knowing it would also be easier to return some day.

Displaced Appalachians were tied together through C&W music and through C&W bars. Occasionally, I was invited to go to a C&W bar with a group from work. It was quite an experience. First, everyone drank copious quantities of beer. The fact that I was underage did not matter; the police were never present and presumably were afraid to enter. With all the beer, there were always fights. I had to constantly be on the lookout for where the drunks were who might start something. I also had to avoid being in the wrong place at the wrong time.

Another consequence of all that beer is that unattractive women began to look pretty good. There was no shortage of women who worked in factories and offices during the day and partied on weekends. Billy Joe, one of my colleagues in the factory, had a theory: "Always date and marry the ugly ones; they will appreciate you a lot more than the pretty ones." I understood where Billy Joe was coming from but never adopted his theory.

In the far rear of the factory was the third section of the factory that most of the workers never visited. It was the galvanizing pit, which literally was a pit of molten chemicals for galvanizing the steel couplings we put on the fiberglass rods. The chemicals were noxious; it had to be one of the more unhealthy places to work and made our section of the factory nice by comparison.

The galvanizing work was done almost exclusively by Mexicans. There was one white guy who only Sweeney talked to. Everyone else was Mexican, and most were illegal immigrants. During the winter (when I was not there), I was told U.S. Immigration officials occasionally surrounded the factory and rounded up the illegal immigrants. It would take a week or so for the staffing in the pit to get back to normal with other Mexicans. This was more than 40 years ago.

The only reason for me to go to the back of the factory by the galvanizing pit was to drop off UPS packages for pickup. When I worked in shipping, I would have to walk by the pit to the UPS drop-off location. The Mexicans would watch and whistle at me, which was an insult, in hopes of distracting me or getting me to show irritation. Sweeney told me they were testing me, and that I should pretend not to hear the whistles. So I ignored the whistles, and, eventually, the Mexicans accepted me and the whistles stopped.

There were two brothers who graduated high school and worked in the factory. They both maintained that they intended to work there for a while, save some money, and then get better jobs. They maintained the same story through the several years I worked there.

One of the brothers, Tom, who helped Sweeney in the winter when I was in school, became friendly with one of the Mexicans. One day Tom told me he and I had been invited to play handball with two of the Mexicans the next weekend at a YMCA. I played handball in college and thought it would be fun to play. The following Saturday, Tom and I drove to a big YMCA in Chicago, met two guys (I don't remember their names), and played handball. Despite our relative youth and energy, Tom and I lost badly. The Mexicans were really good.

After handball, Tom and I were invited to go with the Mexicans to their local neighborhood bar. When we entered, everyone stared at us. I soon realized we were the only Anglos in the bar. After we were seated and it was clear we were the guests of two Mexican guys, one by one everybody in the bar came over to welcome us and introduce himself. Then they bought our table a round of drinks. We remained there for several hours. All afternoon and evening, whenever someone entered the bar, they immediately noticed us, ascertained we were guests, and came over and bought us a round of drinks. We were truly guests of the neighborhood.

There were no women in the bar. Either it was improper for Mexican women to be in a bar or the women were back in Mexico. I know it was customary for the men to take jobs and send the money back to their families in Mexico. It was amazing to me that men who worked at terrible jobs and had so little spending money insisted on buying drinks for their Anglo guests. It was their form of hospitality. Today, when I listen to the debate about illegal Mexicans in the U.S., I recall the guys working in the galvanizing pit where Americans would not, and the kind hospitality I experienced in that bar. The U.S. needs to find a way to accommodate the people who contribute to our society and our economy by doing the undesirable jobs that are needed to support the rest of us.

When I first began working at the factory, Jim Miller was the president. Mr. Miller knew the names of each worker and would stop by to inquire about family or hobbies whenever he was on the floor. Everyone liked and, more importantly, respected Mr. Miller; they felt he appreciated them.

When Mr. Miller retired, Bud McKay became president. Mr. McKay was the engineer who invented the production process. He was frequently on the floor tinkering with one machine or another, asking the workers' advice on what worked well and what needed improvement. By the time I started working there every summer, each part of the production process had been improved in some fashion by Mr. McKay working with the guys on the floor.

Despite Chicago's oppressive summertime heat and humidity and the added heat of the factory ovens, Mr. Miller and Mr. McKay always wore white shirts and ties. They set the standard by example for a professional work environment, even in this gritty factory wedged between the train tracks and the truck access in Cicero, Illinois.

A big company in St. Louis, Joslyn Enterprises, eventually purchased the factory. Joslyn sent its own engineers to the factory, and they rarely ventured outside the air-conditioned offices to the steamy, dirty, and odor-filled factory floor. Occasionally, one would come onto the floor and complain to the foreman about something. Sometimes they would make a change, but never with any input from the guys who ran the equipment and the changes were never successful.

The factory ran better with Mr. Miller and Mr. McKay. I learned a lot watching Mr. Miller and Mr. McKay, and I learned a lot watching the Joslyn guys miss the opportunity to continue the improvements.

The factory allowed me to earn enough money for a college education. It paid for my first car, and it provided many valuable lessons of life. I owe much to men and women at the factory, Mr. Miller and Mr. McKay, the production line guys, Sweeney, and even the Mexicans working in the galvanizing pit. My days at the factory were filled with dirty, repetitious work, breathing foul air, and sweating through the high humidity of Chicago's summers. But they were also filled with many valuable lessons that served me well in later life.

Chapter 7

THE LAND DEVELOPMENT LOAN MATURES

As I streamlined operations at Investa and attacked corporate silos, I was also determined to lead and motivate employees while downsizing the company. Early work experiences had taught me valuable lessons in relating to and leading employees, but leadership does not make debt disappear. We were still saddled with unsustainable levels of debt. One of our loans was a $650 million facility with ANZ Bank (ANZ) secured by Investa's land holdings. The loan was to mature in February 2009. We called it the MOF (multi-operating facility).

In late 2008, the GFC had begun, and banks were focused on reducing their outstanding real estate loan books. Land loans were considered the most risky and least desired.

The spring weather provided a sunny backdrop to our tour of the development sites we owned, which were security for our MOF loan. The senior land development executives, Lloyd Jenkins and Cameron Holt, and I were looking at an open field – we called it a paddock in Australia. Someday, according to our project manager, this paddock would be a neighborhood filled with homes and common areas. It was hard to visualize; no other houses were within sight.

My mobile phone buzzed. It was George Giovas, senior banker with ANZ. The bank was the sole lender to our land business, and the $650 million loan was due in a few months. We did not have the money to pay it off.

George had been the real estate lending head for ANZ for several years and knew the ins and outs of the bank and what they would do. He was of Greek descent, medium stature, with black hair and a Mediterranean look; he was also passionate in his beliefs. I started the conversation. "Hi, George. I am out looking at our properties. How are you?"

"Scott, I have just met with the head of our risk committee. We will not get approval to extend the Investa loan. You need to pay it off."

"George, we don't have the money," I replied. "You will have to get an extension."

"That is just not possible, Scott. You will have to ask Morgan Stanley for the money."

"Morgan Stanley does not have the money," I said. "Have you been reading the newspapers?"

George paused for a moment and then continued. "We are going into a possible depression; the bank regulators are all over us. The head of the board's risk committee hates land. There is no way we will get a new $650 million loan approved with a bunch of empty paddocks as our security. It is not going to happen. Just find the money, Scott. You have three months."

I was frustrated. George and I were talking past each other. I finally exclaimed, "I am standing in the middle of a very big and very empty paddock. This place has no homes anywhere in sight. We have no water, no utilities, and not much in the way of roads. This place is so remote, we don't even have cows on it. George, you do not want to own this place. Trust me. And we have other fields like this. We just need time."

George was persistent. "Scott, the bank needs to exit the land business."

Finally, I was losing patience. "George, you cannot exit the land business, and you will be in it more than you ever imagined if you do not extend this loan. You will have thousands of lots and acres on your balance sheet. And don't forget, this loan is cross-collateralized with $3.7 billion of other Investa loans. You put us in default on this one, and you are looking at a Centro-scale bankruptcy and all the related stress on the banking system. There has to be another way."

George stepped back from the confrontation and replied, "We'll talk when you return to Sydney."

A week later my mobile phone rang. It was Friday night, which is an unusual time for a business call, and I was at a cocktail party for the American Club. The caller ID read George Giovas. I stepped out of the room while answering.

"Hi, George. How's it going?"

"Scott," he said. "Have you talked to the Morgan Stanley guys in New York?"

I responded, "Not today. What's up?"

George said, "Gary Newman, ANZ's head of institutional banking, just called me. All deals are off. Our senior guys met with Morgan Stanley real estate guys in New York, and the meeting did not go well. Any possible deal to refinance Investa's land loan is dead."

Unless I could convince the bank executives to change their mind, Investa was dead. Without the ability to pay off the loan when it matured, Investa would be considered insolvent and not permitted to do any further business.

I was shocked and needed time to find out more information. "George, I will call Chris Niehaus in New York tomorrow morning; they're all asleep now. We have to refinance the loan; we both know this. I'll see what happened and I'll call you over the weekend. Please see if you can get more color on the meeting."

At 6 a.m. the next morning, Saturday in Sydney but only Friday afternoon in New York, I called Chris Niehaus in New York.

"Chris, it's Scott. What happened at the ANZ meeting in New York? The bank is on the warpath. If they don't refinance the land business, we are dead."

Chris replied, "Sorry to hear that, Scott, but not surprised. One of our senior lending guys and I met with Gary and a couple of other guys from the bank. Our guy was a little aggressive pushing the bank to make concessions, and the ANZ executives may have interpreted what he said as not intending to pay back the existing loan."

"Chris, that is crazy," I said. "The loans here are recourse; we cannot give the keys back as you can in the U.S. and the Morgan Stanley funds have loan guarantees; all our debt is cross-collateralized. How could you guys threaten the bank? This is just nuts."

Chris understood my concern but also lived within the then-pressurized environment of Morgan Stanley. He replied to me, "Everyone here has been under a lot of pressure. We have bad loans all over the world and have had to take some tough positions on many of them. See what we need to do to get the relationship back on track. I'll fly down if you need me to participate in meetings."

That afternoon I called George.

"George, it's Scott. We screwed up. Some things were said or implied in New York that do not reflect the relationship we have with the bank. I'm sorry. We need to set up a peace meeting between Morgan Stanley and ANZ. It is in both companies' interest to repair the relationship. If you can get your guys to the table, I will bring an executive team down from Morgan Stanley. They are under lots of strain and pressure."

"Will they apologize?" George asked.

"Yes," I replied.

"I'll see Gary Monday and will let you know."

A few weeks later, we assembled after work in a private dining room at the Japanese restaurant, Azuma, in Sydney's Chifley Towers. The room was made to look very Japanese, including small cups and chopsticks at each setting and rice paper hangings adorning the walls. Even the attentive staff was Japanese. The setting felt intimate, despite the fact it was located in the shopping arcade of a Sydney office tower.

Gary Newman was the host, and George Giovas and James Amati, our relationship banker, attended from ANZ. Gary is an experienced banker with 30 years in the business and tours in Asia and Australia. He is a bear of a man, with grey hair and a rumpled look. He speaks with conviction and years of experience and is not hesitant to express his informed opinions. He was the head of institutional banking for ANZ and a key decision maker for corporate lending.

Steve Harker, CEO of Morgan Stanley Bank Australia, Hoke Slaughter, Asian head of MSREF from Hong Kong, and Chris Niehaus from New York joined me. Steve is an old hand with many years of experience showing in his thinning grey hair. He remains trim in figure, and often speaks in an earthy vernacular, reflecting his earlier days as a union organizer and Labor Party activist.

Hoke is a polished Morgan Stanley executive with an Ivy League pedigree and decades as a successful banker. He carries a very tall and commanding presence. Hoke oversees Morgan Stanley's real estate investments in Asia. This was a meeting of seasoned executives with years of experience dealing with challenges and issues throughout the world but also with no shortage of opinions and egos.

This was to be the peacemaking between MS and ANZ. The dinner was critical; failure to restore the relationship would likely mean the demise of Investa and possibly the Morgan Stanley funds business.

Gary had pre-ordered the food. Unfortunately for me, Gary had recently adopted an extremely health-conscious diet and preferred raw sushi and sashimi dishes; in contrast, I believe all meat should be thoroughly cooked. I believe there is a reason why cavemen discovered fire – so they would not have to eat raw meat.

The first dinner course was served: raw something. Everyone ate and talked about the emerging GFC; I talked some and pushed around my food looking without success for a place to dump it. If only I had sat near the potted plant. Everyone else finished but the waiters would not clear until I was finished eating. Finally, I ate some of the slimy grub, and the plates were cleared.

I felt okay. I would survive. Maybe I would have a parasite eating my insides out, but modern medicine would hopefully save me from death.

The next course was served: more raw meat. The conversation was going well; it would not look good if I puked. I ate some more, and the plates were cleared.

The next course came: more raw meat. Finally I turned to George next to me, "Doesn't this place cook anything?"

George and James stifled the urge to laugh. They knew how painful it was for me to pretend I liked the uncooked potentially bacteria-filled, parasite-laden morsels, and yet we were making progress on working together and even talking about future deals.

Finally, dinner ended. Negotiations to refinance the land business were back on the agenda. I survived the uncooked food without illness or parasites.

At the end of the dinner, we agreed to work together. ANZ would work through Investa instead of dealing direct with Morgan Stanley for the time being. Gary warned that the land loan would have difficulty being approved, and encouraged the Morgan Stanley guys to find money from somewhere to pay it off. MSREF did not have much money, but they had some.

We eventually negotiated a deal with ANZ. We would pay down the loan by about $200 million and then reduce the outstanding balance over the next three years in specified increments. I used part of the money I negotiated with Sonny at our first meeting to do this.

The deal was made ever more difficult because Morgan Stanley was under pressure during the GFC, and the attorneys in New York needed to approve what we were doing but were far removed from our operations and local banking conditions. The attorneys constantly questioned our actions, demanding detailed rationale and explanations.

As time grew short and the loan maturity date approached, Chris Niehaus called me at home.

"Scott, we have lots of lawyers here working on the Investa loan. There continue to be issues; you need to be in the loop, given the possible consequences. You need to be part of our conference call. We have our next call Wednesday."

"What time?"

"Unfortunately it is late morning in New York and late afternoon in London. That means it is in the middle of the night in Sydney [actually 2:30 a.m.]."

"Great. I am not sleeping much anyway so it doesn't matter."

The finance negotiations were also complicated by our need for cash to pay operating costs and debt service. The market for selling office buildings was closed; nothing was selling because there were no buyers. So we had to sell land, including finished lots, to people buying homes, larger parcels to homebuilders and developers, and even entire projects to competitors. Lloyd Jenkins called the situation "the company's dash for cash." As we were negotiating the loan refinancing with ANZ, the list of our land assets was diminishing. Still, we needed to assure the bank we were committed to grow the business over time.

Over the next few weeks, the attorneys, Ming Long, our treasurer, and Jonathan Callaghan documented the new loan. However, time was growing short. At one juncture, we needed a Morgan Stanley official to sign a document authorizing us to sign preliminary documents or the bank was unwilling to proceed. This issue arose suddenly and demanded an immediate response.

I called Chris Tynan of Morgan Stanley's Sydney office.

"Chris, we need an officer of Morgan Stanley to sign the preliminary documents ASAP."

"Jay Mantz in New York is the only one who can sign."

"Okay, Chris, let's call him right now."

"Scott, let me call Lori, who is the in-house attorney and she can explain it to Jay. Stay on the line."

"Lori, we need Jay to sign the document we sent earlier today. It is really important."

"Jay just left the office – it is midnight here. Can it wait until tomorrow?"

"No, do you know where he went?"

"Yes, he is having a late dinner in the city."

"Will you please take the document to him and get it signed?"

"Chris, do you mean you want me to go to the restaurant, interrupt Jay's dinner at midnight, and ask him to sign a document?"

"Yes, and then could you please scan and email it back to us tonight?"

"Sure, what the hell. All they can do is fire me and maybe that would not be so bad."

Later, Chris Tynan called.

"Jay signed and it will be sent in an hour."

"Thanks, Chris. Well done. It looks like we survive to fight yet another day."

Between the late-night and early-morning calls with Morgan Stanley, there was little time to sleep. I tried to go to the gym after work as often as possible; I had few outlets from the pressures of work and exercise was a needed tonic to avoid another health relapse.

On weekends, when I was not immersed with divorce pleadings, I often went for long walks to clear my head. Favorite routes were over the Harbor Bridge through the Botanical Gardens, often ending up at the art gallery. Sometimes, I would stop in a church like the old Anglican Church off Elizabeth Street near our office in Sydney and just sit and take in the peacefulness.

I worried that the stresses in my life would result in a health relapse and a stroke like the one that killed my father. Medication for my cholesterol and blood pressure helped, but I was still concerned.

Chapter 8

COLLEGE:
THE GREAT ESCAPE

When I enrolled at Indiana University in 1965, I had no idea I would become a businessman, much less be dealing with banks and potential corporate insolvency.

It was always understood that I would go to college and I would pay my way, which limited my options. I applied to two schools: the University of Illinois and Indiana University. Most of the better students from my high school went to U of I (Illinois), so I went to IU (Indiana). I always wanted to be a bit different and take less well-travelled paths, exploring and encountering new people and experiencing new adventures. At IU, tuition was affordable ($15 per credit hour), room and board was cheap, and my sister, Margot, had gone there and liked it.

The campus was characterized by a beautiful collection of natural limestone buildings constructed with stone taken from nearby quarries. The majestic stone buildings were complemented by flowers and seasonally flowering trees that benefited from Southern Indiana's fertile soil and long growing season. Indiana University in Bloomington, Indiana, is a beautiful and serene setting for studying and learning.

I was unprepared for college. My motivation was to get away from home, and I had given little thought to studies, future plans, or anything else. During my freshman year I lived in one of the oldest dorms, Wright Quadrangle. My roommate was a reclusive chemistry major, who was a junior and somewhat anti-social. We did not have anything in common and did not communicate much. Because of my mismatched experience, I marvel at Davidson College's elaborate room-mate-matching process that benefited both of my sons.

I developed good friendships with other dorm mates; there were several music majors who were fun to be with. No one studied much, and two of my better friends flunked out after first semester. I was too smart to flunk classes, but I clearly reveled in my freedom and was more focused on winning the dorm bridge tournament (which I did) than excelling in school.

I learned to play bridge as a youngster; my mother loved to play and needed a partner, so she taught her children. After Judy, Bing, and Margot grew up and moved away, I became the designated partner.

At IU, my favorite bridge partner was another student, Byron, who was blind. We used braille cards, which gave us an advantage whenever Byron dealt the cards. No one ever questioned Byron's uncanny ability to guess where the opponents' key cards were. They may have wondered at times, but were not about to suggest being blind was an advantage.

I lived cheaply, but so did many of my dorm mates. We ate at the dorm and did not spend much money. I do not recall having a job at college my first year; my savings from the factory and minimalist spending habits allowed me to get by until I resumed work at the factory during various school breaks.

Social life at IU revolved around fraternities. I joined Pi Kappa Alpha (PiKA), which appeared to have some reasonably intelligent members, as compared to most of the fraternities I visited. During my second year, I lived at the fraternity as required, studied little, and worked first as a waiter, then as steward for the fraternity. Waiters received free room and board, and the steward received room and board and a small payment for overseeing the kitchen and meals for the fraternity.

My biggest challenge as steward – I was responsible for all the meals – was dealing with our cook, Opal. Opal was a very large, overweight woman who was missing a couple of teeth and did not look like

an accomplished cook, but she provided hearty meals to hungry, indis-
criminating college students. She spoke with a Southern drawl, never
clearly articulating her words. Consequently, she could be hard to understand at times for a "Northern boy."

Opal was also stubborn; she did what she wanted to do and did
not appreciate direction from college students or anyone else. She never
went to college and may not have attended high school either. I think
she resented the relative affluence of college students compared to her
impoverished surroundings.

Once when the delivery guy did not give Opal what she wanted, she announced just before dinner that there was nothing to eat. I
scoured the kitchen looking for anything edible. Finally, I found some
pancake batter and announced we were having pancakes for dinner. She
thought that was absurd – pancakes were for breakfast and not dinner
– but she agreed to cook them because we had nothing else. Eventually,
Opal and I figured out how to get along – generally she did what she
wanted and I didn't object.

On Sunday afternoons, we often served steaks and fraternity
members were allowed to invite dates for this once-a-week sit-down
meal. Opal only cooked steaks well done; she did not seem to have the
ability or willingness to try medium or rare. Finally, I bought some plastic pieces marked "rare," "medium" and "well done." If a diner ordered
"rare," we would just insert the corresponding plastic tag in the steak
and serve it. Eventually, everyone learned that all steaks were well done
but they had fun pondering whether to order rare or medium.

I did not enjoy fraternity life. The house was old, and the sleeping
porch was unheated and freezing in the winter. In addition, the bathroom was in poor condition and overcrowded, and the brothers had
little interest in intellectual discussion. Living in the fraternity also cost
money; my nonexistent spending habits didn't work as well living amid
brothers with more resources than I had, and who were always doing
things that cost money.

I was active in campus politics and joined the student Tryus Party. During one election I convinced a guy from one of the biggest fraternities on campus to run for office, thinking that with the support of his fraternity and the generally low-voter participation, we would win a key seat. I put up signs in the district, "Vote for Mike, the Man with the Plan." A couple of days later, Mike called and complained. "Everyone is asking what my plan is. What do I tell them?" Mike had no plan or the ability to create one. I learned that having a good candidate is critical to winning an election. Fortunately, Mike lost when he forgot to tell his fraternity members they were supposed to vote.

I continued to be interested in politics and public policy. I wanted to change the world and make it a better place through personal engagement. I think my aspirations were similar to many of my political science colleagues in the 1960s.

At the end of every summer, I would give my mother half of my savings from the factory. She would add some of her own savings, and give it all to a friend, John McHugh, who was a successful stockbroker in Chicago. John had a soft spot in his heart for Mother and her struggle to raise a family on limited resources. As a result, he would take the money from Mother and buy hot IPOs (initial public offerings) when they were issued and sell them soon thereafter when the shares rose in price. John used a small part of his allocation of IPOs that otherwise would have gone to his best customers. In this way, I was able to supplement my wages with a few hundred dollars each year.

During my sophomore year, I called Mother before the end of the first semester and asked her to send me my wages and any earnings from John McHugh so I could pay second-semester tuition. I remember the call vividly, even though it was many years ago. She began to weep and finally explained that the IPO crashed, and we lost all the money. I cried, too. One-half of all the money I earned from working in a steamy, chemical-filled factory in Cicero was gone. I was completely broke. I almost quit school then.

Instead, I went to the financial aid office of the university and explained my plight. I knew Mother would never agree to fill out a financial statement; her financial situation was for her to know only, and she was not about to share her plight with anyone else. Fortunately, the university understood and arranged for me to receive a National Defense loan, backed by the federal government. It took me years to pay off the loan, but I still appreciate having been able to secure a loan to continue college. Without a student loan, I would have been unable to finish my degree.

After another summer in the factory, I returned to IU for my junior year. I was still depressed. I never had any extra money, I was having trouble with acne, my social life was lousy, and I knew lots of people but had few good friends. I really did not fit with the fraternity crowd nor did I fit with the dorm crowd. After another semester, I had enough. I quit college in the middle of my junior year, returned home, and resumed working at the factory.

I expected Mother to berate me for yet another failure, but she surprised me by expressing sympathy. I never understood the change in attitude, and have wondered about her out-of-character attitude many times since. Only much later, when I was listening to tapes my mother made about her life did I learn how she came to understand my un-happiness and need for a break from school. On the tape, she talks about going to the University of Arkansas for one semester, pledging a sorority, and then realizing she was too broke to keep up with her new friends. She left school and never had the resources or time to return. She knew what I was feeling.

Making money has never been a goal or primary objective in my life despite growing up without much. I wanted to make a sufficient income to pay my modest bills but was otherwise driven by values and a desire to excel. At some point, I realized achieving success in business provided money, and having money was better than not having it.

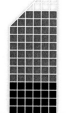

Chapter 9

THE LAND DEVELOPMENT LOAN MATURES (CONTINUED)

Usually, when a borrower and a bank agree on a loan, a short period to document the agreement follows, but there is no suspense. The parties agree on a closing date to sign the documents, and the deal takes place as planned. This is how it has always worked in my experience, but not with Investa in 2009.

When all the documents to refinance the land development loan were ready, we scheduled a time with the bank to meet and execute the deal. I believe the agreed time was 9 a.m. on a Monday in March, 2009. The documents had been prepared and laid out neatly at the lawyer's office, awaiting execution.

That morning, I awoke at 6 a.m., as usual, turned on my Black-Berry and noted an email from Chris Niehaus. "Scott, please call me as soon as possible." The implied urgency was a bit unusual, but I called Chris as requested.

Chris responded with a sense of urgency, "Scott, do not sign the loan documents."

I exclaimed in disbelief, "What? Are you nuts? Do you know how hard this deal was to get through ANZ credit approval? We walk on this deal, and we are out of business."

Chris remained calm. "I understand your concern. We just need some more time here. We need a clean audit opinion before we take on any new debt facility or we may face personal liability."

"Chris, I am very familiar with personal liability in Australia. I meet with outside insolvency lawyers regularly to discuss our situation. I am potentially personally at risk. Believe me, you and your colleagues in New York are okay; I would not do anything that puts you or others at risk. I need to sign the documents."

"Scott," he replied, "do not sign those documents. We have issues here. You must not execute."

"What if I just sign them anyway?" I asked.

"That would not be a good thing," he replied forcefully.

I said good-bye and hung up. I sent an email to Jonathan Callaghan, my general counsel; Ming Long, treasurer; and Graham Monk, CFO.

"Please meet me at the office ASAP. Morgan Stanley is telling us not to sign the docs."

I called Paul Bartlett of ANZ, who had taken over the deal from George Giovas. Paul was a seasoned banker with years of experience before joining ANZ the previous year. The novelty of the situation would be an early test of our new relationship, and I was worried that Paul did not have the insights into the ANZ decision structure to help navigate a potentially dangerous situation. It was too early for Paul to be at work; I really did not want to talk to him until I collected my thoughts and leaving a voice mail was easier.

"Paul, it's Scott. I hope you are doing well. We have had a hiccup from New York that we need to work through, and I can't sign the documents today. We should be fine next week. Hope this does not cause a problem. Please call me if you have questions."

At about 8:15 a.m., Paul called back. "Scott, you must sign the documents today. This deal was almost impossible to get approved. Mike Smith, our CEO, had to overrule the head of the Risk Committee. We cannot afford a delay or this deal could go away. You need to sign fast."

"I understand," I responded. "But the lawyers in New York are insisting we need additional approvals there before we can sign any loan documents. Sorry."

"James and I are coming over to your office right now. This is really serious."

Later that morning, my phone rang. It was George Giovas. "Scott, Gary Newman wants you in his office in 15 minutes. Don't be late."

Fortunately, it was only a 10-minute walk.

"Scott, what the hell is going on?" demanded Gary. "Never in my 30 years of banking has a borrower not shown for a closing. The explanation had better be good."

"Gary, Morgan Stanley is under a lot of pressure and government supervision; they have lawyers everywhere. They have some kind of an internal legal problem. They need a week to fix it."

Gary was frustrated. "Scott, you have exactly one week. If you do not close within the next week, we are pulling the loan and putting you in default. Is that clear?"

I felt a moment of relief. "Yes. Thank you, Gary. I really appreciate the time and willingness to let us work through the problem."

"One week. No more," Gary said firmly.

One week later, closing was set for 9 a.m. at the same lawyer's office. The night before the rescheduled closing we had a video call with the Morgan Stanley team in New York. Jay Mantz conducted the meeting, but there seemed to be more lawyers in the room in New York than business people. We were officially given approval to sign the loan documents when Jay asked, "If anyone has an objection, say it now. Otherwise Scott is signing the documents tomorrow morning."

No one objected. What a sense of relief after living on the edge all week wondering if we needed to put the company in administration and close the doors.

The next morning, I turned on my BlackBerry and scanned the many overnight messages. One was from Chris Niehaus: "Scott, please call me as soon as possible."

Was this some kind of a joke? I took a shower and dressed. Maybe another email would arrive saying "no need to call" while I was getting ready for work. I was on the video call late last night and heard everyone say we were good to sign. Maybe I should pretend I did not receive the email. No, it could not be that bad. I called Chris back.

"Scott, we have had another problem come up," Chris began. "You cannot sign the documents. We need a few more days."

I was in complete disbelief. "Chris, the show is over. We're dead. No more time. It's over."

"Scott, do what you can," he said. "We had arranged a bank loan to the funds, and that provided the auditor sufficient headroom to sign the accounts. But the loan has not been executed and the bank CEO is out of town. The treasurer can execute, but the documents are not finalized. We just need more time."

"I'll call ANZ," I replied, "but I expect we're finished. I'll let you know."

"Sorry, Scott."

I called Paul Bartlett again and left a voice mail. It was déjà vu in the most unpleasant way.

"Paul, it's Scott. We need to talk as soon as possible. Ming and I can come to your office, or we can meet in the coffee shop of our building. This cannot wait. The news is not good."

Paul returned my call a few minutes later. "James Amati and I will meet you in the coffee shop in 20 minutes."

In the coffee shop, I tried to explain. "Morgan Stanley needs to secure some kind of loan which has been approved but is not documented. They expect it will be done within the next two days, but I don't believe anything I hear anymore about timetables. We need to extend closing."

Paul was not sympathetic. "We can't. You need to close. You heard Gary."

"Paul," I said. "I cannot ask you to extend closing; I realize this. You need to ask me to extend closing."

"Why the hell would we do that?" he asked.

"I don't know," I responded. "Maybe because the world is going down, and we want to live another day. Having Investa crash and burn is not good for anyone. It's bad for the bank, the investors, the employees, our careers, the community, the economy; it's a disaster for everyone. We need to figure out something that's outside the box."

No one spoke. We all were considering the dire consequences of what was happening.

Then James Amati, the relationship manager with ANZ and the youngest person at the table, ended the silence.

"There may be something. There was a recent Supreme Court ruling about the enforceability of security clauses in loan documents. The bank is in a frenzy to find out what the clauses say in all of our loan agreements. We could ask for a delay so we can review the clauses in this document."

"James, great idea but it would take a couple of hours to review the documents," said Ming.

"Not really." James said. "We would have to find the pertinent clauses, copy them, send them to internal legal for review, request an opinion in writing, and review the opinion to make sure we agree. Then, if there needed to be changes, we would need to work with you."

"How long would this take?" I asked.

Paul interrupted. "As long as you need, within reason. You know how lawyers can drag things out, even simple things."

I asked, "Will the bank request a delay in closing?"

Paul responded, "We need to talk with George and Gary, but it seems prudent, and we may even win a few points within the bank for being alert to this issue."

The bank requested an extension later that day. Documents were signed a week later after we agreed to a minor change regarding security provisions, and MSREF received its new loan commitment.

The ANZ land loan was subsequently paid down over time as required and was never at risk of default. It was refinanced again two years later and continued to be a successful loan that funded Investa's substantial land development portfolio and generated good fees to the bank.

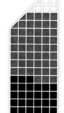

Chapter 10

THE MARINES: DEFENDING CALIFORNIA

The path to Australia was a circuitous one for me. Joining the U.S. Marine Corps when I was 20 years old was a wrong turn but provided a different set of lessons to help me confront future challenges. Dealing with unhappy and threatening bankers was easy when compared to Marine Corps drill instructors.

After I dropped out of college, I resumed working in the factory. It was 1968, and the Vietnam War was at its peak. My draft number was 20 out of 365, so there was no doubt I would be drafted when the Selective Service learned I was no longer in college.

At the factory, Tom occasionally would tell tales from his time in the Marine Corps. The Marines seemed to be a special group, an elite and storied fighting force. If I was going to war, I figured it would be better to go with the Marines than with the Army. Both services were drafting and both accepted two-year enlistments, so I enlisted in the Marines.

My stint in the Marines was served in California instead of Vietnam, but it was a dark chapter in my life. Basic training was very tough physically and mentally. I learned I could take constant abuse without breaking, run miles farther than I ever thought was possible, and surmount obstacles which I never dreamed I could. I learned that I had internal resources that I did not know I had; if I could survive boot camp, I could survive anything. In a perverse way, the Marines gave me self-confidence I lacked previously and made me understand that conditions at college and at home were not that bad compared to the alternative.

I believe everyone has vast internal resources and abilities they do not realize. Unfortunately, the only way to appreciate fully the strength of these resources is in time of crisis.

Each recruit platoon had three drill instructors, who were incredibly tough and demanding. One occasionally showed a flash of empathy, one responded to every question or incident with demands for pushups and physical exercise, and one was to be feared more than anyone previously experienced or encountered. Sergeant Ware, an imposing, tall, muscular black man would often stand toe-to-toe with recruits yelling and cussing and threatening anyone who did not perform as desired. We all were very afraid of Sgt. Ware.

I also learned what the phrase "beat the shit out of" meant. One night Sgt. Ware called (more like whispered my name), and I did not hear him. Finally, another recruit rushed up and told me the drill instructor was waiting for me in back of the tents where there was no light or visibility. I was clearly in trouble and afraid of what was about to happen.

"You did not come when I called you," Sgt. Ware explained in a menacing tone.

"Sir, I did not hear you," I replied without conviction.

"Did I tell you to talk?"

"No, sir."

Then he pushed me against a wall and slugged me so hard he literally knocked a piece of shit right out of me. I was the example that night to the platoon of what happens when you don't hear a command.

About four weeks into basic training in San Diego, I incurred a severe knee injury during a run through the obstacle course. As we traversed the monkey bars, swinging from bar to bar, the recruit in front of me lost momentum and came to a dead stop, hanging from one of the bars. I crashed into him, and we both fell to the ground far below. He landed on my knee, tearing the cartilage and a ligament. My military career was over.

Initially there was great pain, followed by discomfort and swelling. I managed to limp after the platoon to mess and back to the barracks, hiding the pain, but not the inability to walk. The next morning my knee was the size of a grapefruit, and it was almost impossible to walk. The drill instructor told me to go to the infirmary. It took me a couple of hours to walk about one half-mile, but I finally made it.

The doctor looked at my knee and knew my days of running through obstacle courses were over. I was given a bed in the infirmary, a pair of crutches, and my knee was drained for the first (but not the last) time using a six-inch needle to suck out excess fluids. About a week later, I was reassigned to a light duty recruit platoon where drill instructors still yelled at the recruits but physical exercise was prohibited.

I needed an operation at the nearby San Diego Naval Hospital, but the hospital was full of injured sailors and Marines from Vietnam. Providing treatment to an injured recruit was a low priority, so I remained on the recruit base for months. Much of that time I was assigned as the secretary and clerk to the recruit motivation platoon. Boot camp was very hard; the verbal and physical abuse was ever constant, and some recruits broke down mentally. They could not continue. These recruits were assigned to the Motivation Platoon. Quickly, I realized the drill instructors in the Motivation Platoon were determined to force these "unworthy" candidates out of the Marine Corps. This was accomplished by increasing stress levels to the point of causing complete mental breakdowns. Virtually every day, recruits would literally go crazy, jumping out of a window, attempting suicide, or they would just become blathering idiots and were sent somewhere "off base," probably to a mental ward at the hospital, where they were processed for medical discharge. As long as I stayed focused on typing reports, filing, and maintaining a low profile, I was not subject to any of this tyranny, although it raged all around me.

Finally, months after my injury, I was transferred to the hospital. I was given a cot in the orthopedics ward and was operated on soon after my arrival. The night of my operation, which was major surgery involving transplanting a muscle where the ligament had withered, and cleaning out the cartilage, I awoke in great pain. The doctor had neglected to write down pain medication on my chart. Also, the nurse, who was a naval lieutenant, had little regard for a private's request to call the doctor and ask him for a prescription. The most difficult night of my life was that night, filled with waves of pain and no relief.

The next day, the doctor was furious that I had not received any pain medication and prescribed two days of morphine. The morphine was wonderful; I know how people can become hooked on narcotics. Then they took away the morphine and gave me pain pills that were much less effective but not addictive. Years later, I still remember the pleasure of morphine, which took away my pain completely.

I had a full leg cast extending from the bottom of my foot to the top of my thigh, but that did not stop the Marines from assigning me to the recruit rehab platoon at the hospital. My first assignment, when I reported on my crutches, was to sweep streets around the base. It was not easy on crutches, but I was a lowly private and, therefore, rated the least desirable assignment. I swept streets for a few weeks and learned to have a healthy dislike for anyone who smoked. The number of cigarette butts that I had to clean up numbered in the thousands. I still resent seeing a smoker casually throw a cigarette butt on a sidewalk or street and expect someone else to clean it up. My memories of picking up all those butts with a broom and pan are not that dim.

I quickly concluded that I needed another job, and the only way to get another job was to make friends with important people. The dispatching hut, which assigned recruits their tasks, was run by a naval boatswain's mate. This is the guy who works his way up from manual labor on ships to supervising manual tasks like cleaning the decks of ships. It takes little brains but considerable toughness.

One day I was assigned to a work detail unloading trucks at the mess hall, which was not easy on crutches, but I learned to adjust. I negotiated for several boxes of cereal before leaving and dropped off the booty at the dispatch hut. Soon, I had a job in the hut, sending others to do the work. I would negotiate with whoever called and requested workers for various goods. The mess hall was the best place to negotiate, because no one missed a few boxes or cans of food, and the senior enlisted guys running the place were used to making deals. We could not negotiate with officers who requested work details, however, and they were always the most demanding and condescending. We always sent the most invalid of recruits to those assignments to spite the officers. The senior enlisted guys there understood the situation, but the officers were furious.

The Marines lost my pay records when I moved to the hospital, and I was completely broke. I needed money, if just to buy a Coke now and then. I tried various strategies to make some money. My most successful was fortune telling. I found a book in the base library that explained how to read palms and tell fortunes. I charged 50 cents and split the proceeds with the boatswain's mate who ran the dispatch hut. The sailors and Marines were not particularly smart, and my fortune-telling ability was soon highly regarded and widely known around the base. The business stayed good for the remainder of my stay, as new patients rotated in, and old customers rotated out on a frequent basis.

My least successful venture was cutting hair. Another guy and I bought a hair clipper from someone who was moving on to another assignment. I marketed the business, especially to recruits who had little spending money and were willing to take a chance on a cheap haircut. The problem was that my buddy, the cutter, had a terrible sense of straight and even. We only did crew cuts, but it was important to have the hair at one level. Ridges on a crew cut did not look good. Almost everyone we cut left the hut bald. Indian, his nickname, would cut the hair lower and lower trying to even out his rows until he finally ran out of hair. If we had stayed in the business, we both would have been beaten or killed by our unhappy customers.

I shared the hut with the boatswain's mate, an Indian (I actually think he could have been a mix of black and white parents but told everyone he was an Indian), a very nice, fat, black guy named Willie, who was hospitalized for being overweight, and another guy, David Trotter, who endeared himself to everyone using what little money he had to buy candy bars and then giving them away to either make friends or acquire subsequent influence. It was an odd group, but we made the most of our lives at that time.

We played low stakes poker at night (quarter ante). Whenever I was losing too much (e.g., a couple of dollars), I would drop out. I had little and could not afford to lose much. One day, Willie started losing and kept playing, thinking he could recoup his losses. At the end of the evening, he had lost his entire monthly paycheck. He cried; his wife and three children were counting on that paycheck to live on. I felt terrible for Willie and I learned another lesson: never bet what you cannot afford to lose.

The hospital base was occupied mostly by sailors and Marines who had been injured in Vietnam, and there were many people who were not normal. Maybe the stress of Vietnam caused behavioral problems. I am unsure, but I knew one always had to be careful, especially a private, the lowest rank, and the one to pick on if someone more senior had personal problems that needed to be blamed on someone else. One night, Willie, Indian, Trotter, and I were sitting in the hut and an angry boatswain's mate (not our guy) came into the hut looking for trouble. He immediately started goading Willie, calling him names, and demeaning him. Willie was a gentle man and no match for an angry, liquored boatswain's mate. Finally, I stepped in to protect Willie, knowing I was sure to get beaten, but Willie was a friend who needed help. The boatswain's mate came at me but before he reached me, Indian jumped on his back and Trotter tackled his feet, sending Bots down with a crash. Then Willie, all 350 pounds of him, sat on Bots until the MPs came and took him away. That night I learned true friends are those willing to risk personal well-being to help someone else.

Each year there was a Marine-Navy football game at the hospital. Unfortunately for the Marines, they were typically badly injured while many of the sailors seemed in pretty good shape. I had my crutches and cast but was still drafted to be on the Marine team. That was how desperate the team was that day. The Navy had a big fullback, who ran through the Marine defense at will. Finally, the coach sent me in as middle linebacker and told me to stop the big fullback. The next play he ran at me and I hit him hard with one of my crutches, causing a fumble. That was my play. The coach took me out, realizing they would kill me if he put me in again. But we were both pleased with the results.

When the Marines finally agreed that I was enlisted and deserved to get paid, they initiated a temporary pay of $20 per month until they sorted out my records, which was not done until after I was discharged. With some money, I was able to take advantage of a couple of weekends of liberty. One weekend I went to Tijuana with a group of Marines. Mother had sent me one set of civilian clothes; I never asked her for any money because I knew she needed her money.

Tijuana was filled with bars, prostitutes, soldiers, and sailors on leave. There were prostitute auctions at some places and propositions for sex on almost every block. I had never been to such a place. Fortunately, I only had enough money to buy a few beers and return to the base. The fact that my military ID card said in big print, "Not authorized to visit Mexico," did not matter when I crossed the border. I suspect the military police at the border had the same restrictions on their cards.

Another trip was to Los Angeles over a three-day weekend. I got a ride with Bots, but I didn't have much money to spend. I just wanted to see L.A. I spent the first night sleeping in the bus station. It was pretty uncomfortable, and I did not sleep much. The second night, I bought a ticket to an all-night pornographic cinema because it was open and inexpensive, thinking I could sleep in the darkness. The L.A. police came in every couple of hours to check for vagrants (it was illegal to sleep in a movie theatre then); sleep remained difficult.

Finally, I met another down-and-out guy, and we split the cost of a low-quality transient hotel room. The next day I returned to the Naval Hospital, unimpressed with L.A. from the vantage point of a temporarily homeless person.

After several months at the Naval Hospital, a naval officer, in preparation for a medical discharge, interviewed me. They removed my cast, but my knee was very weak and had no range of motion. The doctor told me to be prepared to walk with a limp the rest of my life. There was no question I would receive an honorable discharge with medical conditions, but there was a question about benefits. At the time, I was considered 20 percent disabled; at 30 percent disabled I would have automatically been entitled to full education benefits, including college tuition and room and board. Between 10 and 30 percent disability, these benefits were provided at the discretion of the discharging officer based on his or her evaluation of the disability and its effect on future career opportunities. My hearing officer was wearing a college ring with a PiKA on it. When I told him I was a fellow fraternity brother, it was decided that I needed the educational benefits. I think that was the only time I actually found a benefit in having joined a fraternity. Had I not been a PiKA, I most likely would have received the same benefits, but it may have been a longer conversation.

I was sent back to the recruit base before final discharge. I worked as a clerk for a month or so, still subject to verbal abuse because I had not graduated from boot camp. Finally, in late fall, I was discharged.

I never thought I would be happy to return home, but I was then. I realized there were places worse than home and much worse than college. After suffering almost a year as a Marine recruit, I knew I could withstand any pressure and any setbacks; nothing could be worse than the year I spent between 1968 and 1969.

Upon my return home, I was determined to rebuild my damaged knee. I would wake up before dawn, proceed to the nearby forest preserve in North Riverside, and force myself to run. At first I could only run a few steps because of the pain. Eventually, I was able to run miles. This was the start of almost 30 years of running, until my knee finally gave out in Houston.

After my run, I would shower and go to work at the factory. I worked there until the second semester of school started at IU, when I re-enrolled and resumed my education, partly courtesy of the U.S. Veterans Administration (VA).

Chapter 11

THE SALE PORTFOLIO OFFICE LOAN MATURITY APPROACHES, THE CFO RESIGNS

Refinancing Investa's land loan in March 2009 brought a temporary sense of relief, but we were quickly confronted with an even greater challenge. Investa had another $650 million loan secured by a handful of office buildings; we called it the Sale Portfolio loan. The value of the underlying portfolio had declined to a level below the outstanding loan balance. The loan was to mature on June 5, 2009, at 11 a.m. The banking syndicate consisted of nine banks, including European, Asian, and Australian banks. The biggest lender, Hypo Bank from Germany, was insolvent and had been taken over by the German government.

Despite the obvious risks of default and considerable obstacles to surviving the loan maturity date, I felt we would find a way through the ominous path ahead. Perhaps it was surviving Marine Corps boot camp, rebuilding my knee after doctors were so pessimistic, or overcoming other personal obstacles, that I remained optimistic despite what seemed like overwhelming odds.

I called Chris Niehaus early in the process well before the loan maturity date.

"Chris, we have started working on the Sale Portfolio loan; it is going to be really difficult. I will need to draw all the remaining promised equity to pay down the debt balance – the loan is now about 110 percent of the underlying asset values. Even then, the banks do not like this loan, especially the foreign banks."

"What can we do to help, Scott?"

"I need someone from Morgan Stanley to work with the foreign banks; we do not know these guys, they all want out of Australia, and we have no influence other than the threat of mutual destruction if we default. The loan is cross-defaulted with the $3 billion Hold Portfolio loan."

"Okay, Scott. We will get a senior finance guy involved. He is CFO for MSREF Asia and put the original deal together. He knows the banks as well as anyone."

The new finance guru came down to Australia a couple weeks later and met with Jonathan, Graham, Ming, and me to discuss the loan. He was an American of Chinese decent. He looked Chinese, was short in stature, dressed in perfectly tailored suits and spoke in crisp American-accented English. He was a very smart guy with insights on each bank, key people to be concerned with, and lending strategies. He was also a friendly guy, offering encouragement and appreciation for the progress we were making with the local banks.

Unfortunately, after two trips to Australia and several bank meetings, he was taken off the Investa assignment. MSREF was dealing with issues all over the world, and our guy was no longer available to us in Australia. Finally, I called Chris Niehaus in New York.

"Chris, it's Scott. We really need to have your finance guy working for us. We are reaching a critical stage in bank discussions. We can work on the Australian banks and Ming and Jonathan have formed a relationship with Hypo Bank in Germany, but what about the other banks?"

"He is not available. We will get Peter Ireland involved, a New Zealander from the investment banking side. He is a good guy."

"This is serious. We put your guy out there and then he disappears and someone named Peter, a Kiwi, shows up without detailed knowledge of Investa or the loan syndicate. This does not feel right. We are at great risk here. I met with outside counsel this week, and his advice was that we were skating very close to the edge of insolvency under Australian law."

"Scott, Peter should be helpful; otherwise you and Graham Monk (Investa CFO) will have to make do."

Soon afterwards at Suncorp's offices in Brisbane, Graham Monk and I met with John Debenham and Mark Baker from Suncorp. Suncorp was a participating lender in the Sale Portfolio loan but had announced it was withdrawing from corporate lending and multi-lender facilities like our loan facility. Graham and I knew that convincing them to stay in the Sale Portfolio lender group was going to be an uphill challenge.

Graham made the introductions. "John and Mark, thanks for meeting with us. I want to introduce Scott MacDonald, our CEO. We also want to thank you for the support you have shown us in the past."

John responded, "You're welcome, Graham; we have great respect for Investa and our past dealings. Unfortunately, we are pulling back to Queensland, and are withdrawing from lending in New South Wales."

I said, "We appreciate that, John, but you are a lender in the Sale Portfolio loan, which matures in a few months, and we need you to stay in that facility. We are having trouble holding all the foreign banks, and if they saw an Australian bank withdraw, they would withdraw, too. The loan would default and would bring down the $3 billion Hold loan with it because the two loans are cross-defaulted. I think you would agree this would be catastrophic for the industry."

"It would definitely be unfortunate," John replied, "but we have a relatively small piece of the loan and have other issues we need to focus on, so we will not be staying in the refinance."

"John, we cannot agree to this," I said, trying to sound very convincing. "The economy is fragile; we need to refinance this facility or there could be dire consequences beyond Investa."

"Scott, we are not going to participate in the refinance," he said with great conviction. "No matter how you ask the question, my first answer is 'no,' my second answer is 'no,' and my third answer is 'no.' What don't you understand?"

Graham seemed to be turning a bit white; he was not used to confrontation with lenders.

I responded. "John, your first three answers do not work, so we need to start working on the fourth."

John replied, "I think this meeting is over."

A few weeks later in my office on a Friday afternoon, Graham Monk came in.

"Scott, after careful consideration, I have decided to resign from Investa. I cannot tolerate how close the company flirts with insolvency. My reputation and my personal resources are at risk if the company does not make it. Sorry, but I cannot stay here."

"Graham, you cannot resign in the middle of trying to refinance the Sale Portfolio. The banks will kill us. The CFO bails out right before a big loan is to mature. We are dead. I do not accept your resignation."

Graham had clearly thought about what he was about to say and would not be deterred. "Scott, I am resigning from all boards and my CFO position. You cannot stop me."

"Graham, look, it is Friday afternoon," I said. "Please give me until Monday morning to figure something out. We will date the resignation from the boards effective today after close of business so you are not at risk. Please, I need a couple of days."

"Okay," Graham replied. "I will resign as CFO Monday and from the boards after close of business today."

I called Chris Niehaus that night and left a voice mail.

"Chris, it's Scott. Graham Monk just resigned. It's the middle of the night in New York, but you and the guys can think about things while I try to sleep. This is a disaster. First, your lead finance guy disappears and then our CFO quits. The banks will not have confidence to go ahead with a refinance; they will suspect things are amiss."

At 5 a.m. Saturday morning after a sleepless night, I called Chris in New York. It was Friday afternoon there.

"Chris, it's Scott. I haven't slept all night. I am meeting Campbell Hanan tomorrow morning to see if he knows another potential CFO, but frankly no one who is any good would take this job without having the refinance completed. There is just too much risk. I figure you guys still have $200-$250 million in dry powder. We may need $650 million the way things are going."

"Scott," Chris replied. "We don't have any more money. The cabinet is bare. You have what Sonny promised and what the Special Situations fund will match, and that's all there is. We are restructuring or giving back loans all over the world. Things are really grim here."

"Scott, what can you do?" he asked.

"Our only option," I said, "is for Ming Long, our treasurer, to step up, and she and I will take on the banks. Peter Ireland will continue to work behind the scenes and Graham will stay on as an employee and help where he can. His contract calls for a six-month notice, and he is a class guy and will honor it. I will try to spin a reason why he is leaving and not have it due to fears that we are insolvent."

"Good luck," Chris said and the call ended.

Monday morning in my office, I met with Graham.

"Graham, here is what I have been thinking. It would look really bad for you personally and for the company to have you abruptly resign. The banks would think we have had a falling out or there were irreconcilable differences. Here is what I would like you to consider.

"First, you are retiring from Investa. The last few years have been challenging and you have decided it is time to relax, play some golf and perhaps find some cushy board seats.

"Second, you have agreed to stay on at Investa through the Sale Portfolio refinancing to make sure it gets done.

"And third, after the refinancing, you have agreed to sign a contract with Investa to supervise our Kooindah Waters Golf Resort, where you have a second home. This will help us fill a need – the resort needs attention – and works with your desire to play more golf and work fewer hours.

"What do you think?"

Graham was surprised; this was not something he contemplated. "Where did you dream up this one? Me, as supervisor of a golf resort? Give me a break. But it is intriguing; as you know, I do not believe we are managing that resort correctly."

"Then you will do it?" I asked.

"I will think about it overnight and tell you tomorrow," Graham replied.

"It's a deal," I said with more hope than conviction.

The next day Graham Monk agreed to my offer, including assuming management responsibility for Kooindah Resort, working with our team there. His subsequent tenure resulted in a significant increase in financial performance of the resort. More importantly, however, the banks thought the whole scenario made good sense and respected Graham's desire for a less intense job. I think they all envied him.

Throughout my career when confronted with problems and negotiations, I always look for "win-win" solutions, where all participants realize benefit. The Kooindah solution for Graham allowed him to reduce his exposure to a possible Investa default while keeping him in the Investa family and leveraging his experience to help us with our resort.

But we still had to refinance the Sale Portfolio loan or we were out of business.

Chapter 12

COLLEGE: PART 2

In 1969, it was hard to imagine becoming a successful corporate leader someday. I returned home after receiving my discharge from the Marines and resumed working in the factory. My bad knee did not function very well, and every morning I rose early and went to the nearby forest preserve and forced myself to run despite the pain. The Marines taught me to endure pain and overcome obstacles, and I was determined to walk without a limp when I returned to college.

After Christmas, I returned to IU in January, 1969, and resumed my college education. This time I was motivated to learn, and received As instead of Bs and Cs. However, I was still very low on money.

I needed a car and Tom, my friend in the factory, told me about a local bank that often had repossessed cars from borrowers who defaulted on their loans. I went there one day and met with the manager. He had the most beautiful and cool 1967 dark-blue Chevrolet Camaro convertible; I wanted to buy it so badly. I had $1,500 in savings and offered it all. The manager tried to negotiate, but I did not have any more money. Finally, he gave up, and I bought my first car for $1,500, which represented all of my savings from the Marines and the factory.

Returning to IU, I drove to Bloomington in my newly acquired Camaro and stopped for gas just outside of town at the Clark petrol or gas station. I met a guy, Smitty, working in the gas station, and I asked him about any places to stay nearby that were inexpensive. I also needed a job.

I wound up getting a job at the gas station; in those days gas stations did not offer self-service. Pumping gas was not much different than the repetitive routine of working in the factory, but I was able to interact with new and different people and being outside was far better than being in the confined factory space. The gas station job was dull, but conversing with the wide variety of people who stopped by was always interesting. For some reason, people expected gas station guys to know stuff. I am unsure why anyone would have such an expectation. "Where's the best place to …?" Or "Where can I find some cute college coeds?" If I knew I would be there myself. Occasionally, someone driving an expensive sports car would ask if I could loan him some money for gas. I thought that was a pretty funny request, and always declined with a smile.

I also moved into a freestanding trailer with Smitty. If you have ever driven through rural areas, you must have seen occasional trailers plopped down in a field and maybe wondered who would live in such a place. I did.

Smitty was an interesting character, similar in some respects to the factory guys I had worked with in Cicero but with a rural flavor and outlook. He was big-boned, overweight, and uneducated in the formal sense. He offered a sloppy look with a beer belly hanging over his big belt, but he also had "street smarts," which kept him out of serious trouble, and a good sense of humor, especially when it came to parodying college "snobs."

I lived in the trailer with Smitty until the pipes froze. I could deal with the field mice, which shared the trailer with Smitty and me. I could accept the various crawling creatures that wandered into the trailer, but was very wary of the big and often colorful spiders. However, I could not deal with the lack of water. Eventually, I moved out and into a low-rent trailer park on the south side of Bloomington. I continued to work at the gas station and remained friendly with Smitty.

On weekends, I would occasionally join him as he visited local C&W bars. There was a major separation of town and gown in Bloomington. Students and faculty did not venture into "Townie" or "Cutter" (a term describing local stone quarry workers) places and vice versa. However, with Smitty, I passed as a town person and was accepted in the local bars.

Bloomington's C&W scene was much like the places I went to with the factory guys who were from Appalachia. Everyone drank large quantities of beer, fights always broke out, and unattractive girls looked truly beautiful as the time passed. One night I was sitting at a table with Smitty and a couple of his friends when someone at another table broke a beer bottle on the head of the man next to me (at an adjacent table). There was blood and fists flying everywhere. Smitty was sober enough to grab me and head for the exit. As we drove away, a parade of police cars with lights flashing and sirens whining passed us headed for the bar.

I was involved in a number of college-sponsored activities during my time at Indiana. Initially, I was active in local campus politics, served in the model United Nations, and was elected to the mock Senate. I continued to be keenly interested in politics and was determined to make the world a better place.

After my return to school, I learned about a black man who was running for mayor of Bloomington. No black person had ever been elected in Bloomington, which still had a Southern flavor and obvious racism outside the college campus. Someone in one of my classes was an older black woman (let's call her Josie, although I do not recall her name), who was working on his campaign while raising her family and studying for her bachelor's degree. My interest in politics, involvement, and helping others fit well with this long-shot election effort. I joined the campaign and became very involved in its organization.

When our candidate began to make progress, the death threats began. There were remnants of the Ku Klux Klan in Bloomington, and signs left on homes along with late-night threatening telephone calls terrorized our black campaign workers, particularly. It was on this campaign, I witnessed the fear that comes from racial hatred. Josie was particularly scared after an anonymous caller threatened her children. At campaign meetings, we would count the attendees to determine if anyone was missing. Earlier, white campaign workers in Mississippi had been killed supporting a black's quest for elected office there, and we were nervous.

As our candidate made progress, our excitement was tinged with fear of unknown consequences. Despite the harassment tactics, our candidate won. Today, it is no big deal for a black man to run for office, but back then it was a major event. In the process, I developed intolerance for any form, however subtle, of racial discrimination.

At IU I was invited to join the Student Foundation, which consisted of students who were viewed as future leaders. Members worked to make IU a better place. Because I had spent time with Smitty and worked on the mayoral campaign, I had a greater familiarity with issues affecting local people who were not related to the university.

I put together a plan to go to the greater community, with emphasis on the university community, and request donations of books that were gathering dust on shelves, but would be used and valued by the greatly underfunded local public and school libraries. With eager support from the local librarians and funding and support from the Student Foundation and its director, Curt Simic, we received thousands of donated books. It was the greatest surge of books into the local library system's history. The librarians sorted through all of the books, and any they did not want we shipped to rural libraries in Appalachia. I knew from my factory buddies that books were not easily found in rural schools and libraries in the mountains. The campaign was a big success, and I was interviewed on Indianapolis television.

Subsequently, I put together a voter registration drive, but it was controversial and never received full funding or support by the foundation. Some thought it was a political act aimed at helping my candidate for mayor, which may have been partly – but not completely – true. Unlike the book campaign, the voter registration effort was not particularly successful.

During the summer breaks, I worked in the factory. After my third year at IU, however, I secured a summer job working for the public aid (i.e., welfare) department in Chicago as a caseworker. Because the pay was not great, I also worked the evening shift at the factory. The welfare job started at 7:30 a.m. and ended at 3:30 p.m. when I drove as fast as I could to the factory, changed into a T-shirt and jeans, and worked the shift from 4:00 p.m. to midnight. I did not get much sleep that summer, but it was a rewarding experience in broadening my understanding of social welfare issues and understanding the challenges of urban poverty.

I found casework very challenging and frustrating. No matter how hard I tried to improve people's lives and provide access to opportunity, I was unable to reach most of my clients in a meaningful way. One family had a teenage son and daughter who were hanging around the projects without work or something constructive to do. They both told me they wanted jobs but could not find anything available. I called employers throughout the area and finally secured job interviews for both. Neither showed up for their respective interviews; they told me they overslept. I learned they really did not want to work and that work and a more structured and punctual lifestyle was not viewed positively in their social setting.

Another time I visited a woman's apartment for the first time and knocked on the door, which went unanswered. There was a boy – probably 10 years old – playing nearby and he was clearly watching me. When I went to leave, believing the woman was not at home, the boy went to the door and pounded it much harder than I had knocked. She opened the door in response, as he knew she would.

The boy was her son, but when I asked why he was not in school, she replied that he was too stupid and the school did not want him.

After returning to the office, I grabbed her voluminous file and read it carefully. The boy was not stupid; he was deaf. He needed a hearing aid. He had been tested, but had never received the hearing aid.

I followed up and made arrangements for the mother to take her son to the doctor for tests and to be fitted for a hearing aid. I called the day before to remind and even arranged for a taxi to take them. There would be no charge; the public aid department would pay the bill directly. Unfortunately, the woman and her son never showed. Something else came up and she had other priorities, which may have involved drugs or alcohol. When I finished the summer, the boy still had not received a hearing aid and a senior permanent caseworker tried to assure me that she would follow up; I was skeptical. The caseloads were so large, no one in the office had time to deal with the truly difficult and needy cases.

I decided my future was not casework but trying to change and improve society at a higher level. I was not sufficiently patient to suffer the challenges imposed by individuals who lived with a different value system and culture that discouraged success and achievement. It truly was part of a never-ending cycle of poverty, and I had difficulty dealing with this realization and my powerlessness to change it.

My last year and a half at IU was very different than my first years there. After the Marines, I was focused, more confident, and better funded. As an official disabled veteran, the U.S. government paid for my tuition, books, and direct school expenses. I had to pay my living expenses and rent, but I was able to enjoy school without working at time-consuming menial jobs. In recent years, I have donated money to Davidson College, The University of North Carolina, and Indiana University so needy students don't have to do menial work to pay for their living expenses. I know the value of a little money to a broke student; it makes a huge difference in one's ability to enjoy college.

Unfortunately, I developed a case of severe eyestrain my last year at IU. I assume it was due to spending too many hours reading coupled with a "lazy eye" condition where one eye ceases to focus and converge with the other eye. I went to doctors but was told not to read so much and the underlying issue went untreated.

Despite my problems with eyestrain, I still graduated from IU in the spring of 1970. I skipped the actual commencement ceremony; Mother had no interest in going, and I needed to start work in the factory as soon as possible so that I could earn and save money to pay for graduate school. I still had no inclination I would someday be negotiating billion-dollar loans, operating companies in distant countries, and leading hundreds of staff through difficult times.

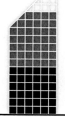

Chapter 13

A MAJOR AUSTRALIAN BANK THREATENS INVESTA'S SURVIVAL

In 2009, the GFC was unfolding, resulting in increasing pressures on banks to reduce their real estate loan exposure. I had resolved Graham's need to resign from Investa, but the $650 million Sale Portfolio loan was still coming due soon, and the banks were resisting efforts to refinance it. Failure to repay or refinance the loan would result in the closure of Investa.

Steve Harker, CEO of Morgan Stanley Bank in Australia, returned my call from earlier in the day around 10 p.m. It was May of 2009 and darkness was coming earlier each day as winter approached. I had been at Investa for about a year, which was characterized by top-to-bottom reorganization and continued crisis management. We had survived the refinancing challenges of the land loan but now faced the maturity of a $650 million office loan; the amount was far more than the portfolio of assets' actual value. It was a challenging time.

"Scott, sorry for the delay in returning your call. What can I do for you?"

"Steve," I replied, "we seem to be putting in place the last touches on a bank syndicate to refinance the Sale Portfolio loan. Executives at CBA [Commonwealth Bank of Australia] have been really difficult. Their risk guys are making the decisions and are not cooperative. They only have a small position in the Sale Portfolio loan, but they have been so difficult to deal with, we agreed to let them out. At the last minute

NAB [National Australia Bank] stepped up and filled the gap. We owe NAB big time.

"However, now we cannot get the documents done by June 5th – which is less than a week away. We asked all the banks for a loan extension to June 30th – a lousy 25 days – to complete the documents. Every bank has said 'yes' but CBA. If CBA does not agree to an extension, we default. It is in CBA's interest to extend, but we have not gotten anywhere. The relationship guys in the bank want to extend; it is the risk guys who have not approved. Do you know someone high up the ladder at CBA we can go to? We are desperate at this point."

"Scott, keep your morning open," Steve responded. "I will make a few calls."

About 11 p.m. Steve called back. "Be in my office tomorrow morning at 9 a.m. A senior risk executive for CBA will be there. You have one shot. If he buys, you get the extension; if he does not hear what he wants to hear, you're dead."

"Who else should I bring with me?" I asked.

"No one. This is between you, me, and the guy from CBA."

At 9 a.m. the next morning in another Morgan Stanley conference room on the 39th floor of Chifley Tower, a senior risk executive from CBA walked in with two associates. Steve made an introduction and we shook hands but the mood was serious. None of the CBA guys smiled or gave any gesture that could be considered friendly. They declined an offer of coffee. They sat down across the conference table from Steve and me. I had planned for Steve and me to have our backs to the windows and beautiful view of Sydney Harbor so the CBA guys could see the view and maybe lose a bit of concentration. But they ignored the view.

Finally, I made the presentation without notes or materials on Investa's plan to refinance the loan and why it was in CBA's interest to cooperate. I wanted to look directly at them as I talked and try to connect. The senior exec from CBA asked several questions after I finished talking; fortunately I was able to answer them. He then stood up to leave and his two associates sprung to their feet in unison. In response to my request for the extension, he indicated they would approve an extension until June 30 and not a day later. They then walked out. I felt a huge burden had been lifted from my shoulders, if only temporarily.

It was 6 p.m. on June 4th about a week after the meeting with CBA. It was my birthday, but I was in no mood to celebrate. Ming Long and Jonathan Callaghan and I sat in an Investa conference room. We stared at the silent phone. The loan facility agent called to say all the banks but CBA had formally approved the maturity date extension to June 30. However, no one had heard from CBA. I called the CBA risk exec I had met with; Ming called everyone at CBA she had ever met or taken a business card from. The calls went unanswered and unreturned.

The loan would mature the next day. I asked Jonathan at exactly what time; after checking the documents, he told me 11 a.m. No one had ever asked him before at precisely what time of day a loan matured. Without an extension, we were finished. So close and yet so far.

Jonathan asked, "Scott, is this normal?"

"No," I shook my head. "This is not normal."

Finally, Ming shouted with glee; an email arrived indicating CBA approved the extension. The phone finally rang confirming this. We went home. It was my birthday but I just went to bed. I was exhausted.

To pay down the loan to the agreed-upon amount, we used the available Morgan Stanley equity commitment, but we were still $75 million short of what was needed. I met with Michael Cook who was responsible for asset dispositions and special projects months before the loan matured.

"Michael, we need $75 million. What do we own that is not part of the loan pool and is available for us to sell?"

"The only asset is the vacant building on Bligh Street. It is obsolete, the façade is falling off, and the building is hazardous. We bought it years ago with the intention to knock it down and develop a new building, but then the market changed."

"Who would buy such a building?"

"There are two possible buyers but neither moves quickly. The Metro rail system, which may need an expansion site, or Ausgrid, the electrical utility company, which needs an electrical substation. I am talking to both, but negotiations are slow."

"We need the money before June 30. Do whatever you need to do, but we are pretty desperate for that money."

"Okay, I'll see if we can finalize the deal with the utility company. The Metro guys are too slow."

Negotiations with the utility company progressed but time was running out. Fortunately, the city of Sydney suffered two blackouts in the downtown area during the discussions, highlighting the need for more electrical capacity. I joked that the police were looking for a short guy in a black shirt that cut some cables. The building had no value, but a development site in downtown Sydney offered potentially considerable value. We needed $75 million: we had no other resources or access to money. That dilapidated building was our only piggy bank.

Finally, Michael secured the deal. We would sell the site to the utility company for $75 million, but they would have a put right to sell the air rights back to us for $25 million so we could build an office building later. The $75 million was to transfer on June 29th, one day before the funds were required to pay down the maturing loan as part of the refinancing. We held our collective breath and, fortunately, the money transferred just in time.

On my next trip to New York, I bought Michael a small baseball bat and left it on his desk. I told him he was our home-run hitter.

Meanwhile, Ming, Jonathan, attorneys, bankers, and support staff worked around the clock to document the loan agreement. It was more difficult with some European banks overseen by their respective governments who needed to approve any new loan agreement. The loan was to mature at 11 a.m. on June 30. Later, Anni Honicke, head of property lending for DekaBank in Germany, told me she and other lenders talked every day leading up to the loan deadline. "Do you think Investa will make the deadline and not default?" they asked. The answer right up to the last day was "No."

At 11 a.m. on June 30 in the law offices of Allens Arthur Robinson on the 28th floor of Deutsche Bank Place, the extended loan officially matured, but everyone kept working. In the middle of the previous night, one of the lenders, Hypo Bank, changed its name, requiring thousands of pages to be retyped and printed. The deal was finally signed sometime in the afternoon.

The Sale Portfolio loan was subsequently paid off early as assets were sold. Suncorp stayed in the loan syndicate, but CBA did not. NAB became the new facility agent and subsequently refinanced the one remaining unsold asset. However, almost all of the MSREF cash that had been promised in the beginning had now been spent, and we still had the $3 billion Hold Portfolio loan maturity ahead of us.

After the drama of the Sale Portfolio refinancing, I sat down with Ming Long, my treasurer and effectively the acting CFO since Graham resigned. Ming is an Australian with Malaysian parents. She looks Malaysian but has an outgoing personality. She has a booming voice, an incredible work ethic, and a persistence that does not stop until she knows everything and has every problem resolved. She is one of the most talented financial officers I have worked with, but she lacked self-confidence.

"Ming, you did a great job working with me and the team to refinance the Sale Portfolio. Investa needs a permanent CFO now. Do you want to be considered for the role?"

"Thank you; I am honored but I am not sufficiently experienced for such a responsibility. You need a grey-haired guy with years of experience."

Bonita Croft told me this response should have been expected and was typical of many Australian women professionals. They are talented, but did not think they were as capable as more experienced men.

I realized Ming had the talent and drive to be successful, but I needed to convince her. As good as she was, I did not need a CFO who did not think she deserved to be in the role.

I called Lynn Thurber, who is an extremely accomplished and successful woman and explained the situation. Lynn promised to work on Ming without telling her of my call and request.

Then I called Debbie Page, who was on one of our boards and is a very accomplished Australian woman. Debbie readily agreed to work on Ming, assuring me she had frequently encountered such attitudes. Debbie also agreed to keep our discussion confidential and not share it with Ming.

Finally, I began interviews with "grey-haired men" and asked Ming to join me. I knew she would eventually realize she was as good as the outside male candidates.

Months went by as I waited for Ming to raise her hand and ask for the job. Finally, I told her I needed to hire someone and asked again if she wanted to be considered. This time she said "yes" but insisted Morgan Stanley and our board would want someone more experienced. She did not know the board had approved her promotion and was just waiting for me to convince her.

When we promoted Ming, a reporter for *The Australian* newspaper called and asked to do a feature story on Ming because a woman CFO was such a novelty in Australia. I was asked why I promoted her, and my answer was easy: "She was the best candidate."

Chapter 14

UNC: FINDING BLUE HEAVEN

As a senior at Indiana University, my favorite class was urban economics. I considered pursuing an advanced degree in economics, which was my minor at IU, but I concluded that the study of economics had become too mathematical and too theoretical for me. The economics literature was filled with complex econometric models purporting to support someone's theory and equally complex models attempting to disprove the same theory. I have always been attracted to real situations with real people and problems needing solutions. I needed an alternative vocation to economics.

My urban economics professor suggested I consider city planning. Some noteworthy urban economics authors had come from the city planning profession. As I considered my future options, I was very sensitive to federal government regulations regarding veteran benefits. The VA kept a formal list of occupations. Some occupations required a college degree, which was all the VA would support. Other occupations required an advanced degree, which translated into government payment for tuition and books for a master's degree. When I discovered a city planning career required a master's degree according to the VA, my decision was easy.

I applied to several graduate schools based on the reputation of their city planning departments. The University of North Carolina (UNC) in Chapel Hill, North Carolina, had an excellent reputation.

When I received the acceptance letter from UNC, I found a map of the U.S. and looked for North Carolina. I did not know anything about the state, including exactly where it was.

After my father died, my family did not take any vacations. Everyone needed to work during school breaks, and we had no money to go anywhere interesting. Other than my stint with the Marines in California and a junior-high school class trip to New York City and Washington D.C., I had not traveled outside the midwestern United States.

The only insights I had on North Carolina at the time were two: *Time* magazine had an article about a traveling carnival show in North Carolina where an orangutan with boxing gloves would fight all challengers for a modest bet. Evidently, the orangutan was undefeated. Secondly, a professor I knew at IU moved to UNC the summer before I was to start school there. There were no computers or Internet to search for information, and the local library did not feel the need to stock information on a distant, Southern state.

I packed the Camaro in North Riverside, where I lived in a small brick duplex townhouse with my mother during the summer, checked my AAA map, and headed to North Carolina with little knowledge of what lay ahead. Surely, it would be an adventure.

I arrived at UNC the next day and found a snack bar on campus. There I began making calls from the pay telephone to local realtors listed in the yellow pages of the telephone book, asking if they had rental units. After my third unsuccessful call, a beautiful, young coed approached me. She was short in stature but in perfect shape with long blond hair and the warmest smile almost extending to her sparkling blue eyes.

The beauty queen then spoke, with a soft, Southern accent, "Are you Scott?" This was my introduction to UNC, and it signaled my beginning of a new life. My two years at UNC represented a turning point in my life from an unhappy home environment, long days in the factory, poor social and intellectual stimuli, and always being broke. UNC changed my life.

But first, back to the snack bar. The comely coed worked part-time at the Center for Urban Affairs, where the one professor I knew from IU, David Brower, had his office. Dave asked this girl if she knew of any apartments that may be available, because he had a former student from IU (as in up North) coming to UNC. Northern accents were not that common in North Carolina at the time, and the girl wondered if I could be the same person.

I lived with Dave and Lou Ann Brower and their family for a few weeks until I found a roommate (another city planning first-year student) and an apartment. The apartment was near Dave and Lou Ann's suburban single level home in a quiet, tree-lined neighborhood in Chapel Hill, and I spent many evenings at their home. We became very good friends. I babysat for them often and was called over in the wee hours of the morning when Dave took Lou Ann to the hospital for the birth of their daughter, Ann.

Dave and Lou Ann were very special people. Dave, with his big frame, moppy hair, wrinkled shirts, and rumpled sport coats always looked like an aging graduate student full of energy and with an infectious enthusiasm about life. Lou Ann was the quiet, intelligent, insightful observer, always supportive with a warm smile and quick laugh. They became my family in distant North Carolina.

UNC was a special place. Students went out of their way to be nice, especially to strangers who needed assistance. It was impossible to cross campus without saying "hello" to countless students and faculty I didn't know but whom I made eye contact with or otherwise encountered. Southern hospitality and Southern manners were complemented by the warmest smiles I have ever seen. It was a very friendly place.

The department of City and Regional Planning had excellent faculty that worked closely with graduate students. Classes were small (especially compared to Indiana), and discussions were active. Occasionally, the faculty would join the students in a touch football game; on Fridays many of us would go to the local pub for a few beers to close out the week and debate public policy issues or political positions. The students and the faculty were top tier but they were also friendly and mutually supportive.

The VA paid for my tuition and books; I had spending money saved from working in the factory after graduating from Indiana; and I had received a small competitive scholarship from the Frederick Law Olmstead Society. But the costs of living, including Friday night beer and dating the friendly UNC coeds, were quickly consuming my savings. I made an appointment with Jack Parker, the chairman and founder of the department of City and Regional Planning. Jack was a legend in city planning circles; he was considered one of the founders of the city planning movement in the U.S.

Jack welcomed me into his spacious book-lined office. He looked like a professor with white hair, glasses, and an understanding and welcoming demeanor. I knew of his immense reputation, but he made me feel comfortable and seemed keenly interested in me as a person. He insisted I call him "Jack" despite his age and status.

I told Jack that I needed a job at UNC to pay for my apartment and general living expenses. I was used to physical work but would be happy to do research or whatever helped pay for my living costs. He asked several questions and then told me to return the next week.

To complicate matters, I continued to suffer from severe and painful eyestrain, which limited how much I could read. Reading for more than an hour without a long break led to intense strain and severe headaches. Finally, a doctor in Baltimore diagnosed the problem and gave me eye exercises and special glasses to wear my second year, which helped.

When I returned to Jack's office a week later, he had arranged for me to apply for, and I subsequently received, a HUD (U.S. Department of Housing and Urban Development) grant, which provided needed spending money. He did not want me to work that year while at school and knew I was struggling with my eyes; he wanted me to focus on life and studies and not worry about paying bills. For the first time, I was able to enjoy school and not worry about money. It was an amazing and liberating feeling. Every year, I make a donation to the Jack Parker Fund at UNC, which helps support students in the department. I will remember and continue to honor Jack's gift to me until the day I die.

At UNC I emerged from a shell. I was with interesting, intellectual people, I had a terrific social life, my financial needs were taken care of, and I had many friends, especially in our very close-knit department. The days of Mother's drinking, working in the factory, and being broke were generally behind me.

While at UNC, I developed a passion for UNC basketball. The years I spent at Indiana University covered a period in time when IU basketball was very poor. It was the time between two famous coaches, Branch McCracken and Bobby Knight. At UNC, the legendary Dean Smith was the coach, and his nationally competitive teams played a brutal schedule along Tobacco Road each year. The key player when I was there was Bob McAdoo, who was one of the first prominent college players to leave college early for the NBA. My favorite team today is still the UNC Tar Heels basketball team, dating back to my fond memories from living there in the early 70s.

I played basketball on a department team for a time. One night we only had four players show up for a game, and the referee told us we needed five players to start or we would forfeit. In a moment of inspiration (or desperation) we claimed the dog that came with one of our players was our fifth player and suggested the rules did not specify five "human" players. After discussion and debate, we were allowed to play. I suspect we were the only basketball team to compete at UNC with four humans and one dog. The dog was worthless; he fell asleep after tip-off, but he was critical to let us start. Another human player showed up shortly after the game started, and we were able to play most of the game with five humans. I do not remember if we won the game, but we had fun playing and talking about our unusual team many times thereafter.

Early in the season, my repaired knee collapsed as I was jumping for a rebound and I had to go to the veterans hospital in Durham for treatment and crutches. My competitive basketball playing days were over.

At UNC, candidates for master's degrees in city planning were required to complete and submit a comprehensive research paper. I have always been attracted to out-of-the- box innovative thinking, preferring to explore new paths than follow others. For my departmental research paper, I submitted a series of cartoons, poking fun at various research tools and practices. My friends and I waited for the department's response; either I would receive a "high A" or an "F." Fortunately, the faculty reviewers liked the concept and gave me a high grade.

I graduated from UNC in the spring of 1972. I skipped the commencement ceremony because no family was coming, and I had a ticket to Europe for a summer trip before starting work in Washington, D.C. I knew, however, that I had spent two of the best years of my life in Chapel Hill and I will treasure those memories forever.

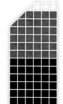

Chapter 15

THE HOLD PORTFOLIO LOAN AND THE TRICK PLAY

After refinancing the land loan and the Sale Portfolio loan, we still had a $3 billion multi-bank syndicated loan facility secured by a portfolio office building assets. The final maturity date of this Hold Portfolio loan was December 5, 2012. Participating banks included Australian banks, European banks, and Asian lenders.

There was an annual valuation test conducted by outside valuers hired by the lenders to assure there was adequate security for the loan balance at the end of each calendar year. The loan balance could not exceed 82.5 percent of total asset values, as of December 31 each year. Failure to meet this test, or LTV covenant as it is called, constituted a default and required immediate payment of the outstanding balance.

Since the loan was originally made, the bank borrowing rates had increased significantly. The spread or margin the banks were charging us was significantly below market. There was no possibility the banks would approve any change in the loan documents or waive any covenants. We could not afford higher margins; we were already losing money. An increase of 1 percent in loan margin would result in an increase in our annual interest expense of $30 million. We just did not have that kind of money.

Several of the participating banks were suffering financial distress and were actively looking for any opportunity to withdraw from Australian loans and repatriate the funds to their home markets. There was virtually no prospect of changing or waiving loan covenants, which required unanimous consent of all the banks.

With the global recession, asset values in Australia had fallen significantly. The loan balance started out at 75 percent of value in 2007 but slipped to 82.4 percent by 2009, narrowly missing being in default. Campbell Hanan and his office colleagues including David Stabback worked incredibly hard to convince independent valuers that our assumptions and forecasts were correct and deserved full value consideration in late 2009; we missed defaulting then by the slimmest of margins.

Unfortunately, property values declined further in 2010, leading to the widespread expectation we would breach the LTV covenant on December 31, 2010. MSREF had access to $100 million by then. We expected that we needed at least $350 million, even if we were able to convince valuers of our internal, more aggressive assumptions.

At one point, we were asked to meet with Citicorp (Citi) bankers. Citi had a small position in the loan. Ming and I met with John Dahl, a senior banker from Hong Kong, who called into the meeting from overseas, and Simon Ransom, head of property investment banking in Australia, who met with us in person.

John got to the point quickly. "There is no way your valuations will be sufficient to meet the Hold Loan covenant, and we all know that Morgan Stanley does not have any money. You will need the consent of all the banks to modify terms of the loan, including Citi. We are prepared to support you under certain conditions."

I replied, "We have not concluded that we will breach the covenant, but please let us know what your conditions are."

"Simon has a list of what assets you will sell and a possible timetable. Citicorp will be your exclusive investment banker and will handle all of your dispositions. We will determine when you will sell what assets and the pricing. If you agree to this arrangement, we will support a waiver of the LTV covenant."

"John, let me be clear," I responded, trying to be firm but not fully convey the anger I felt. Effectively, the bank was trying to take control of Investa and enrich themselves using their small loan position as leverage. "You will not determine what we do or when we do it. It is time for this meeting to end and Simon needs to leave our office, now."

The meeting ended abruptly.

Things were looking very bleak. I flew to New York to meet with the Morgan Stanley team in hopes of finding some additional money.

Sitting in the same conference room where the adventure began, 37B, in Morgan Stanley's offices on Broadway, I made the presentation that we needed more money. We were about to breach the Hold Loan covenants and the banks were not in the mood to give us relief. Time was running short.

The Morgan Stanley senior team was all there except for Sonny Kalsi, who had been put on administrative leave because of an issue in China. He was eventually exonerated, but at that time he was not available to help us.

When I finished my presentation, Jay Mantz responded. "We understand the situation, and we all appreciate what you and your team at Investa have done. But we just do not have any more money."

Then, in a dramatic gesture, Jay stood up, turned his pockets inside out, and said, "Scott, believe me. If I had any money I would give it to you. I just don't have it."

I flew back to Sydney the next day. I knew we were on our own.

When I returned, I called Jonathan Callaghan. Jonathan looked younger than his 40 years. With his perpetually messed brown hair, thin frame, and owlish glasses, he looked like he was still at university. But Jonathan had a sharp legal mind and a creative streak not always found in lawyers who are taught to follow precedent. Jonathan had a terrific work ethic and a desire to succeed. I quickly learned I could trust him, and relied heavily on his advice and guidance. Anything I tasked him with was done quickly, accurately, and professionally. I had an incredibly big task for him now that would test even the most experienced lawyers.

"Jonathan, you need to call a meeting of the best legal minds in Australia, and we need to brainstorm what we could do to solve this problem without using additional money."

Jonathan replied, "I don't understand. How do you reduce the LTV when you keep the loan amount the same and do not pay down the debt?"

"Not sure," I said, "but maybe we can come up with something creative. We cannot sell enough assets to get there – there is insufficient equity to make a big dent in the debt balance. We need an outside-the-box solution."

A week later, the Investa boardroom filled with attorneys and accountants.

"Welcome," I began. "I asked Jonathan and Ming to invite the best and brightest minds to help us think through how we can avoid a loan default. I understand you know the particulars. We need to come up with a creative solution that works within the details of the loan documents. Maybe we can find an argument to interpret a clause to mean we don't have to pay down the debt if the values decline."

After much discussion, it was decided this was not possible.

I asked, "What if someone just forgave the debt? I did a deal once in the U.S. where we loaned someone money and then subsequently forgave the debt."

Generally, the idea was quickly dismissed but someone – I do not remember who – said it would be theoretically possible for a lender to waive their debt and the loan balance would reduce accordingly. This became the kernel of a plan.

Ming called Erryn Lloyd-Jones at BOSI (Bank of Scotland) after the meeting and set up a meeting. BOSI was in the high-risk junior tranche of the Hold loan and more likely to deal than others in less risky senior loan tranches. Erryn came to our office, and we sat in a small conference room to discuss our plan.

Erryn was in his late 30s, black hair, dressed in a dark suit and wearing thick glasses. He projected a rumpled demeanor and would fit comfortably in a crowd. But Erryn was a very creative guy with an open and inquisitive mind. Many bankers just follow established rules and procedures; Erryn was the type to try new things and seek creative solutions to problems.

We discussed a plan whereby BOSI would swap its debt to a friendly lender controlled by us for another loan backed by different security. Then the friendly lender would waive that debt. We did not have much security to offer BOSI, but they were at risk and most likely to lose their investment if we defaulted. By moving them out of the Hold loan stack, we could increase the likelihood BOSI would be insulated from a Hold loan default, which looked increasingly likely, and could possibly be paid off sooner if we survived.

Erryn worried the deal was complicated and unprecedented. BOSI had been taken over by Lloyds Bank of London (Lloyds), which in turn, was partly nationalized by the United Kingdom government. It would be hard to explain to his loan committee in Australia and even more difficult to explain to the Lloyds risk committee in London, who had to approve all new and modified loans. But he said he would pursue the deal.

In consulting Lloyds, many issues arose, including a risky loan Lloyds had made to Morgan Stanley in the United Kingdom. We were afraid the bank was tying approval of our deal to resolution of Morgan Stanley issues in Europe, but eventually Lloyds became satisfied that the United Kingdom loan was going to be okay and did not need to be linked.

Lloyds had a risk committee whose members were not disclosed and not available to meet or be contacted. The bank had set up this "secret" committee to take a hard look at any new proposal without any influence from the originating lender or the borrower. I asked to meet with the committee and was told no one meets with the committee.

Our fate rested with a group of individuals whom we did not know and could not contact.

The day our loan proposal went to the BOSI loan committee in England, I stayed up late at night and waited for Erryn's call as to whether the deal had been approved. I knew Ming and Jonathan were up too; none of us could sleep. We lacked confidence that the secret risk committee would approve such an unprecedented loan when their mandate was to avoid risk. Erryn, our advocate, was a relationship banker in faraway Australia although David Smith, Lloyd's Australian CEO, was supportive and helpful. We were very nervous.

Finally, Erryn received word from England that our deal was approved and called me, knowing I was awake. I sent an email to Ming and Jonathan, not wanting to wake their families late at night. I could hear the cheering in the celebratory emails they immediately sent back.

Ming proposed a similar strategy to Westpac Bank (Westpac), who was also in the junior, high-risk tranche. She proposed that Westpac swap their loan to a friendly lender for the same amount of debt added to an outstanding construction loan we had with Westpac on a newly developed office building. We thought the new building had capacity to carry more debt. Eventually, Westpac agreed.

I called the plan our "trick play." In American football (gridiron), a trick play is a play that catches everyone by surprise and involves tricking the opposition. A trick play is legal, but innovative and unexpected.

The New York lawyers for Morgan Stanley questioned using the term; they were worried our strategy could be interpreted that we were trying to "trick" the lenders, even though they thought our strategy was novel and probably legal. We were not trying to trick the lenders, we were trying to survive and pay the lenders back.

The Morgan Stanley executives were becoming extremely concerned as options were becoming more limited and time to maturity was shortening, but they remained extremely supportive and encouraging. Chris Niehaus had resigned from Morgan Stanley and was no longer available for me to consult. On our prior crises, Chris and I would talk almost daily, brainstorming and sharing ideas.

Hoke Slaughter, the MSREF guy in Hong Kong and a long-time acquaintance of mine, became my sounding board. I had lots of respect for Hoke, but he and I were never close friends like Chris and I had become.

Hoke asked for lots of options and sensitivity analyses throughout the process. Eventually it became clear we only had one viable option left, and it was untested and without precedent. We stopped doing sensitivity analyses when it became obvious that every outcome, other than success of the trick play, would be catastrophic for Investa.

Jonathan engaged outside attorneys to advise us on the legality of what we proposed. They said they thought it was legal but would give no assurances. Lawyers usually rely on precedents, and there were none for our plan.

Jonathan and the outside attorneys were extremely nervous about surviving a possible legal challenge. They both strongly recommended we submit the plan to a Queens Counsel and ask for an opinion. Queens Counsels or "QCs" in Australia are highly esteemed and specially designated lawyers recognized for their expertise and independence. They listen to arguments and give unbiased advice, which is generally respected and followed. Submitting our plan to a QC was rolling the dice with our future, but Jonathan and our outside attorneys were insistent.

We notified the loan facility agent there was a potential legal issue and asked the attorneys representing the lender group be appointed and participate in a QC hearing. One of Australia's top legal firms was engaged to represent the lender group before the QC. We had Freehills, another top law firm, representing us with Jonathan coordinating on our behalf.

The day of the hearing, Jonathan was more nervous than I had ever seen him. He could not stay seated for more than a couple of minutes. He felt the future of Investa was on his shoulders, and there was so much legal uncertainty. I tried to reassure him, although I was nervous, too.

The arguments were made in front of the QC, who asked many questions and took notes. The lenders' lawyers argued against our proposal, pointing out that nothing like this was envisioned in the loan documents, and they maintained it was inconsistent with the spirit and provisions of the agreements. The QC requested that the lawyers all return the following week to his chambers for a decision.

The next week, all the attorneys reassembled before the QC. Jonathan attended; Ming and I stayed in the office, but neither one of us was able to do any work. We sat in Ming's office and talked about everything except the hearing that was going on across town. We were both very nervous. An unfavorable decision almost certainly meant the end of Investa.

According to Jonathan, the QC began his presentation to the assembled lawyers by recognizing the validity of the arguments put forth by the lenders' representatives and showed great sympathy. Jonathan had a sick feeling in his gut; it appeared we would lose.

But then the QC, in a sudden turnabout, said that since our plan was not prohibited in the documents, it must be legal. With that comment, we won. Jonathan returned to the office with the result, and we all felt an incredible sense of relief. We called Hoke, who passed along the message to his colleagues at Morgan Stanley that the Investa team appeared to have dodged another fatal bullet.

Ming and I then met with the major Australian banks, and Ming called the other offshore banks. They did not know our strategy; our deal with all the lawyers was that we would not disclose the issue or QC findings unless we actually implemented our plan. Our message to each lender was that we would deal with the possible loan-to-value covenant breach, trust us and don't ask any questions. We will not ask for your approval, we said. Just sit back and do nothing. The banks did not want us to default but were not able to grant us an exemption or waiver of the covenant without going back through credit approval, and an LTV of

82.5% was about 22.5% above normal and would certainly be rejected. They all wanted to increase their lending margins but were also afraid of the consequences of a big failure. The key to our plan was not asking permission.

In early 2011, we received the final valuations completed as of December 31, 2010. We were in breach of the LTV. The same day, a friendly bank that Ming had identified, recent purchaser of both the BOSI and Westpac Hold debt, notified the facility agent they were extinguishing their debt – just waiving it forever. At first the facility agent did not understand, but Ming explained. Just reduce the amount of outstanding debt, and there will be no breach.

The notice went out that we were in compliance with the LTV and no action was required. We received multiple calls from lenders asking what just happened. One lawyer called and explained the banks intended to insert a new "Investa" clause in future loan documents. We didn't care. We had done what needed to be done, averting disaster through hard work and creativity. In 2011, we correctly believed property values would increase, giving us additional relief from the valuation test.

Subsequently, both the BOSI and Westpac debt were paid in full. For holding the debt for less than a minute and then forgiving the debt, our friendly bank was paid a fee of $1 million, which saved a $3 billion loan from defaulting.

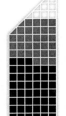

Chapter 16

LIFE AFTER UNIVERSITY

In recent years I have become accustomed to the CEO's office, but my first visit to a business office, as opposed to a doctor's office or school professor's office, does not seem that long ago. My first experience of being in an actual office was when I had an internship in the summer of 1971 between my two years of graduate school at UNC. My summer job was at the National Capitol Planning Commission (NCPC) in Washington, D.C. I was 24 years old before I actually visited an office or worked in one. Before then, my jobs had been in a factory, cutting lawns, or in a grocery store or pharmacy.

The summer at NCPC was another learning experience for me. I worked on the layout of the proposed Metro subway transit system. At a public meeting in Georgetown, I listened to many residents who spoke passionately against having a station in Georgetown because the new transit system would bring so many undesirable people with it. As a result of this narrow-minded opposition, the Metro now travels under Georgetown but there is no station there despite its many visitors. The resulting heavy traffic congestion and pollution is unnecessary, and the shops and restaurants in Georgetown would have benefitted greatly by accessing a larger, more mobile marketplace. This taught me how short-sighted people can be and how difficult it can be to convince people to forego the familiarity of the status quo and their worry about the unknown despite overwhelming and otherwise obvious benefits of change.

After graduating from UNC in May, 1972, I secured a job with Gladstone Associates (Gladstone), a property consulting firm headquartered in Washington, D.C. Upon arriving in Washington, I recall looking in my wallet and finding no dollars. I checked my pockets and had no change. Since I did not have a bank account, I was really and completely broke. I did have a Visa card, a local bank gave me a small credit card advance (I think it was $20), and my roommate loaned me my portion of the first month's rent. I was eager to start work and begin earning money.

My first office was shared with a hyperactive associate named Kevin O'Connell. Our assistant answered the phone, "MacDonald O'Connell," generally leading to confusion, but we had fun with it. We did not have a window; I think our office had been a file room before Kevin and I were hired. My starting salary was $11,500 per year, which I thought was very generous.

At Gladstone we worked very hard, typically spending six days a week in the office, and balancing multiple real estate project feasibility analyses and strategies. I learned an amazing amount of information working for very bright and very driven professionals. It was a wonderful way to start a career.

Our voluminous reports were typed and assembled in a central typing pool, where clerical employees worked days, nights, and Saturdays. There were no computers or fancy word processors in the early 1970s. Reports were typed using electric typewriters; changes and mistakes were accomplished using white-out to cover prior typing and type over. It was a laborious process.

The biggest work backlog was normally on Saturdays, when everyone wanted materials for Monday presentations and meetings. As a new associate, I had no priority or rank and knew I needed help if my reports were to receive attention over more senior members in the firm.

Every Saturday, I began arriving early, making coffee for the typists, and leaving a big box of fresh donuts. I stopped by later and greeted each typist by name. My small gestures were appreciated; most consultants paid no attention to these "nameless" workers. Not surprisingly, my reports and presentations were always in top form Monday mornings while other consultants, including senior officers, often complained their work went unfinished. Once again, my experience at the factory proved how important it was to recognize those who did the work, no matter how low they were in the corporate hierarchy.

There were several young professionals at Gladstone, and we soon began to meet after work on Fridays at a local pub. We shared the pub with guys from CBS News, which was next door, and often saw the leading news journalists having drinks. As a young group of associates in a very demanding work environment, we became very close, bonding and sharing stories about our crazy workloads, personal issues, and life experiences.

I lived in Kalorama, off Columbia Road in Washington, D.C., and walked to work in about 30 minutes. The walk was generally downhill, which was okay even in the humid Washington summers. The walk home at night was more of a challenge, but I was young and excited about life.

At first I shared a furnished apartment with Randy Hodgson, a friend from UNC. Eventually, Randy moved in with his girlfriend (and future wife), Susie, and I rented an unfurnished apartment by myself, also in Kalorama. I did not have sufficient savings to buy furniture, so I bought plywood, foam, and fabric and made my own crude furniture. To size the chairs, I measured my own butt and made the sitting chair wide enough for me. I realized later that heavier people had an issue whenever they used the chair; when they stood up the chair stayed attached to them. Otherwise, I was proud of my homemade, sturdy furnishings.

The apartment was in a transitional part of town that included Latin restaurants, an eclectic group of stores, and a high crime rate. One night I entered the lift in my apartment building, and three young men entered immediately after me. When the door closed, the light went off and one of the intruders shoved me against a wall; I shoved back even more forcefully. Then the light came back on, and I found myself staring down the barrel of a silver revolver. I could see the bullets in their chambers, and I wondered if my life was to end so early. The young gang took my money, but they actually handed back my wallet.

Months later I was walking toward the apartment front door, and a man appeared from the bushes and pressed a gun against my neck. He took my wallet and started to leave, but I was becoming more experienced as a victim. I asked for my wallet back and told him to keep the cash. He hesitated and then tossed me the wallet. The police thought I was nuts, but I was able to keep my wallet with the driver's license, and various identity and credit cards.

Subsequently, a man confronted me with a knife, blocking my way while I was walking down the sidewalk. I smiled; he was too cheap to get a gun and I had acquired a certain expectation on how a robbery should be conducted. I am always looking for "best practices," and I guess I thought poorly of how this altercation was being conducted. I turned and ran, knowing that a knife was not nearly as threatening as being shot.

One morning in my apartment I woke up and stumbled into the bathroom pulling up the toilet seat to pee. There was a splashing sound, and I looked down to see a bat taking a bath in the toilet. I closed the seat, sat down and collected my wits. Finally I opened the seat, lowered a cereal box for the bat to jump in. Then I threw the box out the unscreened window. I remembered my brother Bing putting a bat from my bedroom many years ago into a box; bats must like the confined dark space afforded by a box.

While I was living in Washington, D.C., President Nixon negotiated diplomatic recognition of China, and the government of China leased a floor in a hotel near my apartment for their diplomats until they could set up a formal embassy. One Saturday night a girlfriend and I stopped by the hotel and rode the lift to the China diplomatic floor. Security guards watched every step not sure what to do, but we acted as though we had a reason to be there and were not stopped. On the floor, the hallway was set up with ping-pong tables, and the Chinese were playing. Evidently, the Chinese diplomats were not permitted out of their quarters so they played ping-pong in the hotel hallway for recreation. We looked around and then left quickly before the security guys realized we had no business being there.

I lived in Washington during the Watergate break-in and aftermath, including President Nixon's resignation. It was a remarkable time to live so close to the unraveling of the American presidency and to witness history as it happened. I read *The Washington Post* religiously every morning while walking to work, eager to learn the latest discoveries of the investigation.

I worked on many interesting and challenging assignments, including a financial feasibility analysis for one of the first residential condominium projects in south Florida. One particular project occurred early in my new career. I was part of a multi-disciplinary team of planning and engineer professionals to plan a new community in central New Jersey, not too far from New York City. The team was led by the renowned architecture and planning firm of Llewellyn Davies, which was headquartered in London and New York City. The client was Paul Reichmann and his Canadian company, Olympia & York, who was probably the most well-known quality and visionary property developer at the time. My role was to develop the financial models showing how profitable the project would be.

As the plans took shape, I was struggling with the financial models. I could not figure out how this grand project could make money. I redoubled my efforts, working late nights and weekends but the more I analyzed, the more money the project seemed to lose.

I showed my work to a senior vice president at Gladstone, who shrugged and said it was obviously a bad project and turned to his other assignments, leaving me to deal with the bigger team. I reviewed the numbers with the Llewellyn Davies project director, and he and a smaller team tried different scenarios, but all lost money. The high cost of infrastructure required in the initial stages was never fully offset by the later revenue to be realized.

Finally, the project manager said if I wanted to kill the deal, I would be the one to tell Paul Reichmann he had made a bad investment. No one offered to accompany me; I think they were afraid of the wrath from spending so much with nothing of value as a result.

I flew to Toronto and waited patiently outside Mr. Reichmann's office. I was nervous. I was probably 26 years old and had only worked professionally for a short time. Paul Reichmann was probably the most powerful man in the development industry globally.

Finally, I was escorted into his modest office. He was a fairly thin, Jewish man with a professorial look. He motioned me to sit from behind his desk. He asked why I was there; he was obviously busy.

I explained I had been working on the financial modeling for the New Jersey project and no matter how hard I tried, I could not find a way to develop the property profitably. He asked several specific questions; fortunately I knew the answers.

Then, he stood up, shook my hand and said, "Thank you. I appreciate your effort and your honesty." The meeting was over, and I departed. I later learned it was the first project in which Paul Reichmann lost money.

My world changed once again due to another sudden and tragic death. Two of my closest friends at Gladstone were Jim Curtis and Mary Brown. One day in the fall of 1975, Jim and Mary announced they were getting married. We celebrated at the pub that Friday night; it was a wonderful and memorable evening.

That Thanksgiving, Jim and Mary flew to Indianapolis to share the news with Mary's parents. The returning flight on American Airlines crashed in the mountains of northern Virginia with no survivors.

I was devastated; our small band of young analysts was ripped apart.

Our remaining group flew to upstate New York for Jim's funeral, but the plane was late, so we elected Kevin O'Connell to be the driver because he had no fear and would drive faster than the rest of us would contemplate. It was a wild ride; at one point Kevin actually pulled off the highway and drove over the grass to shortcut the crowded exit ramp. We arrived just before the funeral was to begin; the church was crowded with older people and when we walked in, his parents saw us and began weeping. It was a sad time.

I resigned from Gladstone early the next year; the fun and excitement of going to work had dissipated without Mary and Jim around. Mike Wilburn, who had been a senior vice president at Gladstone, became an executive with W.R. Grace Properties in Philadelphia and offered me a job. I moved to Philadelphia in 1976, 200 years after the Declaration of Independence was signed there.

I only worked in Philadelphia for a year; I did not like the company's bureaucratic approach to land development and thought they were likely to fail after accounting tricks that made results look better than reality became evident.

I also missed a more dynamic social life. In Philadelphia in the 70s, everyone I met still hung with his or her childhood buddies. Not many people moved into or out of town. I didn't care for the social life available there and was glad to leave. By contrast, in Washington, D.C., young professionals were constantly moving in and moving out.

Stephanie, my secretary, guided me through the pitfalls of dating in Philadelphia. When I was interested in a particular girl at work, Stephanie warned me away, "Don't date anyone from a Mafia family," she said. "Mary's father is a big shot. If you mess with her, you will wind up face down in a barrel in South Philadelphia." I thought Stephanie was kidding until I noticed on the local news at night they were always finding dead guys stuffed into barrels in South Philadelphia. I hoped they weren't all pursuing Mary.

I bought my first house in Philadelphia for about $40,000. It was a very small townhouse in a transitional neighborhood near center city on a narrow lane called Naudain Street. Naudain was only wide enough for one narrow car to pass. The townhouse was also narrow and was called a "Trinity house." It had a living room/kitchen on the ground floor, a master bedroom and bathroom on the first floor, and a guest bedroom and bath on the top floor. The three floors were commonly known as the "Father, Son, and Holy Ghost." I sold the house a year later for about the same price for which I purchased it.

After a year in Philadelphia, I joined a friend from UNC, John Slidell, and moved to Annapolis, Maryland, in 1977, when I was 29 years old. John worked at a small consulting firm, ZHA, which needed an additional senior person because of the volume of its business. By that time, I owned real furniture in Philadelphia and needed to move my possessions to Annapolis. I rented a truck from U-Haul but did not know how to drive a manual transmission. Eventually, somewhere between Philadelphia and Annapolis, I figured it out, but it was a bit of a jerky ride.

Annapolis was a beautiful small town when I lived there. It was famous for being the home of the U.S. Naval Academy, but the students were not allowed off campus much, so the town was quiet and slow paced. Many people owned boats, and sailing on the Chesapeake Bay was a terrific way to spend weekends. I bought a small day sailboat (about five meters long with no motor) and often sailed on the weekends.

I also bought a small beach-type house at minimal cost that had been winterized. It was cold in the winter, and mildewed in the summer, but the big picture window overlooked the Magothy River where it entered the Bay and was often filled with colorful sailboats and fishing boats speeding by. The house was a fixer-upper that was never fixed up but its value was an incredible view.

In 1977, I was working on a consulting assignment in Alexandria,

Virginia, and met Jill Weitzen. She was the budget analyst for the city and was responsible for paying my consulting invoices. When I first walked into her office, it was impossible to miss how pretty she was. Her dark brown hair complemented her big brown eyes punctuated by a very mischievous smile. There was a certain excitement about her, an animation found in people who are interested in their work and in the world around them. When I asked to have my invoices paid, she suggested I take her out to dinner. She was not shy either.

I taught an evening class in urban economics at George Washington University (GW) when I lived in Washington, D.C., and some former students of mine worked for the City of Alexandria. They were determined to fix Jill and me up on a date, and they succeeded. That night I saw Jill at a local tavern, which I believe was prearranged by the GW gang.

In contrast to the girls in Annapolis, Jill was the total package. She was smart, attractive, interesting, and fun. I was approaching 30, and the time was right for me to settle down. I had been dating someone else, but I knew right away that Jill was the one for me. I had to convince her. I lived in Annapolis, Maryland, and she lived in Alexandria, Virginia, creating difficult logistics.

That summer I spent a disproportionate amount of time on my little consulting assignment in Alexandria, probably to the detriment of my other consulting assignments elsewhere. Over time, we fell in love, lived together for a while, and then married in August of 1978.

The wedding was quite an event. The ceremony was held in Jill's parents' backyard in East Brunswick, New Jersey. I thought her mother was going to have a heart attack worrying about the decorations, the catering, and the weather. But the wedding came off beautifully. We had a one-man band, who was pretty talented, and after lots of champagne, the attendees probably thought it was a full ensemble. The predicted storms held off to midnight, when most had already left the reception.

Jill did not like Annapolis; she didn't like my small house that was cold in the winter and had a constant smell of mildew. She would get seasick just looking at a sailboat, and was depressed to learn the local grocery store did not even know what a bagel was, much less carry a selection. As a result, we were not destined to stay in Annapolis too long.

When I married Jill, I also inherited her cat, Tinkerbelle. I was never a cat lover, but Tinkerbelle and I soon bonded. Tinkerbelle lived with me in Maryland even when Jill was not there. I remember painting the ceiling one time, and Tinkerbelle watching closely. When I looked down after completing the task, Tinkerbelle had transformed from a grey cat with tiger striping to a grey cat with white polka dots. Fortunately I was able to wash the latex paint off the cat before Jill came home, but it was a battle because Tinkerbelle was not fond of water or baths.

I also created a cat door in a window above the washing machine so Tinkerbelle could come and go as she pleased. Often at night, she would go outside and capture various animals and bring them back to us. Once I awoke to the sound of a fish under the bed. Another time I was awakened by Jill's scream; I thought we were being attacked by a motorcycle gang. Instead, Tinkerbelle had captured a big katydid and let it go under our covers. As the bug moved about, the cat would pounce on the moving form. It must have seemed like great fun.

The work at ZHA was extremely interesting; we specialized in negotiating joint ventures between cities and private developers for urban redevelopment projects. I worked on a number of fascinating projects, including one in Alexandria, Louisiana, which introduced me to the Deep South and central Louisiana in the 1970s.

On my first trip, I met the mayor of Alexandria, who was an old-time politician raised in the tradition of Louisiana.

"Are you a Communist?" he asked me, perhaps because I had a Northern accent.

"No," I replied.

"Are you some kind of a planner?" he asked next.

"Actually I am more interested in working with mayors to implement redevelopment strategies and create jobs and investment in older downtowns. I bet downtown Alexandria used to be a wonderful place."

"Where you all from?" he asked, seeming to warm up a bit.

"My mother was born in Monroe, but the family moved up North in the Depression looking for work," I replied.

From then on, we got along fine. Thankfully, my Mother had been born in Louisiana or I doubt if I would have been accepted.

While I was working in Alexandria, the big local news story was that a former mayor was suing a property developer for failing to pay a bribe when the mayor was in office. The town was divided; the mayor should not have taken the bribe for rezoning the land, but the developer received the better zoning and should have paid as promised.

A new mayor was elected while I was working and was much more engaged and professional. We worked closely together and formed a friendship. After every city council meeting, the new mayor would gather his key aides and me in the back chamber, pull out a jug of locally distilled moonshine, and pass it around. We all felt good after a couple drinks and had some great times listening to embellished stories and jokes.

One time, I needed to catch the last flight out of Alexandria for an important meeting the next morning in Annapolis. I told the mayor I needed to leave by 9:30 p.m. to catch the plane; it was really important.

As the council meeting went on and many people wanted to share opinions on the proposed redevelopment, time grew late and I stood up and started to leave. A big, burly policeman blocked my way and motioned me to sit down. I was not permitted to leave.

After the meeting finally ended way past my flight time, I was distressed, but the same policeman came over and said to go with him. We climbed into the police car and sped to the airport with lights flashing. When we arrived at the runway – we did not bother to stop at the terminal – I was surprised to see a big Delta Air Lines jet guarded by two big policemen. Evidently, the mayor had ordered my plane impounded and refused to let it take off until I arrived. I climbed the stairs and entered the plane trying to avoid the stares of all the passengers. In Louisiana in the 1970s, the mayors had virtually unlimited powers.

Despite my enjoyment and job satisfaction from creating redevelopments in cities suffering from neglect and disinvestment, I did not care for the owners of ZHA. One partner in particular was more focused on maximizing profit than solving problems or servicing clients. Largely because of ethical concerns, I resigned after two years and accepted a job with another consulting firm, Barton-Aschman.

I joined Barton-Aschman's Washington, D.C., office in 1978 and commuted from Annapolis. They wanted me to relocate to their corporate headquarters in Evanston, Illinois. The commute to D.C. for me, and to Alexandria for Jill, was long, and Jill hated Annapolis. So, I accepted the job at Barton-Aschman, and Jill accepted a job with the City of Evanston. We moved shortly after our wedding.

I rented an apartment directly across the street from Evanston's city hall, where Jill was to work. I did not want her to have much of a commute during Chicago's harsh winters. I was only 30 minutes' walk from my office, but I had grown up walking to school in the wintertime and was not concerned.

Evanston evokes many great memories. Work for both of us was interesting. We bought our first home together, suffered through the worst snowfall in Chicago's history, endured the coldest winter in Chicago's history and, most importantly, had our first child there.

Andrew was born in February 1981. Jill and I went to the local cinema, Varsity Theatre, in downtown Evanston, and saw *Lawrence of Arabia*. It was a long movie and after we returned home Jill's water broke, and we were off to Evanston Hospital. When we arrived, the doctor told Jill she was not ready to have the baby, so we walked around the hospital most of the night. We had been to birth classes together and the nurses were great in helping reinforce the breathing techniques and encouraging Jill when the morning came and the delivery approached. Andrew was born on the morning of February 23, and that was the single happiest moment of my life. I had always yearned to be the father I never had, and to be there while he grew into a young man.

Initially Jill had trouble adjusting to being a mother. Subsequently, we learned she was suffering from postpartum depression. I felt the need to fill any parenting gap and spent most nights up with baby Andrew, rocking, singing, and holding him close as he suffered from colic. My song repertory was pretty limited; my two favorites were "This Old Man" and "99 Bottles of Beer on the Wall," but baby Andrew didn't seem to mind. At the same time, I was fighting a series of bouts with strep throat, probably due to stress at work and lack of sleep. The doctor called me "the king of strep throat" because I could not shake it for months. Eventually, we all adjusted and survived.

We bought a house on Ashland Avenue near downtown Evanston. Both Jill and I could walk to work, although she often drove our bright red AMC Pacer that looked more like a moon rover than an automobile. It had been my car in Philadelphia and Jill sold her old Chevy Nova when we moved to Evanston. Eventually, we sold the Pacer and bought a Cadillac Cimarron, which was Cadillac's unsuccessful attempt to produce a moderately priced small car. We felt special about owning a Cadillac, but the car was not very good and needed frequent repairs and maintenance. We did not have a garage, so the car remained in a carport when not in use. That meant it rarely started in the cold winters.

One night, I believe it was our wedding anniversary, we had dinner plans but the car would not start because of the cold. We took a taxi to the restaurant in Evanston. After dinner, we called the taxi company, but were told it was so cold the taxis had all stopped running. That night Jill and I walked home backward into the wind. Our heavy coats blocked the cold winds, but it was one long, cold walk.

Another time, we had friends from Washington, D.C., who came for a weekend visit in the middle of winter. A big snowfall happened that weekend, and when they needed to travel to the airport, there were no taxis running. I called a guy I used frequently to go back and forth to the airport; his name was Fred and his nickname was "fearless Freddie." Freddie could drive through any kind of ice or snow and had never failed to deliver me to the airport or pick me up even in the worst of weather. Freddie agreed to drive our friends to the airport when no one else was willing to try.

Three days later, the weather and streets had cleared and Freddie drove me to the airport. I was surprised to meet my friends still there waiting for a flight. They had remained at the airport hoping to find seats on flights that were supposed to depart without success. Chicago's winters were always challenging, but we enjoyed our life in Evanston.

My consulting projects at Barton-Aschman covered a wide range of issues and geographies. I recall one night I was in Alamogordo, New Mexico, attending a city council meeting with my developer-client, Fred Stuckey, who was requesting a change in zoning for his shopping mall development proposal. I needed to be in Chicago the next morning and the council meeting was running late. Fortunately, Fred had chartered a private plane to take us to Denver after the meeting ended. The meeting went really late, and when it finally ended, the pilot was nowhere to be found. Finally, Fred located him asleep in a nearby motel, and woke him up to fly us out.

We climbed into the little propeller-driven plane in the early hours of the dark morning, and the recently awakened pilot handed us a bottle of Johnnie Walker Scotch and told us to drink it.

"Why?" I asked.

The pilot told us the plane was not pressurized to fly above the surrounding mountains, so we were going to fly through the mountains at night. Fred and I drank the bottle of Scotch. Fortunately, we did not hit any mountains, but we would not have noticed if we had.

After a few successful years, my work at Barton-Aschman was

slowing down. My largest clients were shopping center developers who hired us to undertake financial and market feasibility analyses for proposed new developments. Beginning in the late 1970s and early 1980s, the biggest developers and owners hired staff for these studies instead of consultants. I also did work for cities planning and implementing urban redevelopment strategies, but funding for redevelopment was declining. I realized my business model was not well positioned for the longer term and began looking for a new job in Chicago.

My early professional years provided a good foundation for my future career. I developed research and financial skills, learned real estate fundamentals, studied acquisition strategies and structure, and experienced and dealt with a variety of business conditions and people. No two situations were ever exactly the same, but lessons learned helped prepare me ultimately for confronting the challenges at Investa.

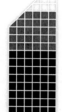

Chapter 17

ACQUIRING A LISTED COMPANY WITH ALMOST NO MONEY

After being on the defensive and in survival mode for so long, an opportunity arose to do something positive at Investa. ING, the big Netherlands-based bank, had decided to exit its global real estate platform, including its suite of listed funds in Australia. Morgan Stanley was ING's investment banker for the transaction, but we managed to have Australia excluded from the Morgan Stanley mandate. In that way, Investa could bid without being conflicted for control of the ING Office fund (IOF), which was listed on the Australian stock exchange.

Investa was a listed company before Morgan Stanley took it private in 2007. We wanted a listed platform and tried a partial IPO in late 2009 without success. I felt we needed a listed fund as a balance to our flagship unlisted fund, Investa Commercial Property fund (ICPF), because it would allow us to access a different capital source for future projects. It also provided us with a possible exit vehicle when Morgan Stanley decided to liquidate its investment in us. So controlling a listed fund was very strategic. The only problem was we didn't have any money.

Chris Green, Brett Robson, and Andrew Scade of Macquarie Bank met with the Investa team and gave us a proposal in 2010. We agreed to submit a bid to take control of the responsible entity, which owned the management rights to IOF. It would be the first opportunity we had to leverage our office skills and add buildings to our management portfolio instead of selling assets.

Oddly, the first obstacle was a colleague in the Sydney office of Morgan Stanley. The senior acquisitions guy wanted to use MSREF funds to support an offer from Mirvac, a bigger Australian real estate investment trust (REIT) and competitor to us, to buy IOF. I called Morgan Stanley executives in Hong Kong and New York and raised hell. How could Morgan Stanley back competition for us in Australia? Either they made a bet with us or they did not. MSREF senior management vetoed participation in the Mirvac proposal even though it was unclear how we would ever pay for any acquisition.

ING wanted proposals to buy all five of their listed funds in one transaction. In addition to IOF, ING owned the rights to IIF (ING Industrial fund), IEF (a small entertainment fund consisting of pubs), ILF (living fund consisting of retirement communities in the U.S. and Australia), and IHF (a fund owning health care facilities).

With Macquarie's guidance, we joined with Goodman, a large industrial property company in Australia, and submitted a joint bid. Goodman would buy the industrial fund for all cash; we would buy the management rights to the other funds and then would liquidate the three smaller funds. Linking with Goodman gave us a strategic advantage over competitors: Goodman was the logical buyer for the industrial fund so ING had to deal with us, too, if they wanted a total funds solution.

Negotiations continued for months. ING seemed to change directions many times. They redefined the process and dates, the data offered on the funds for sale was sketchy and incomplete, and there appeared to be a difference of opinion on how best to proceed between the bank in Amsterdam and the independent board of directors in Sydney. Management wanted to internalize operations of the funds instead of selling the management, thereby retaining their jobs, and the ING board spent millions of dollars advancing the management-takeover plan. There were advisors and lawyers representing the board, who seemed overly concerned about not making mistakes. At times we did not know with whom to negotiate.

Goodman was very aggressive in pursuing its intention to take over ING's industrial fund. They could be because the company was cashed up and had other financial partners. If ING did not cooperate, Goodman could turn up the heat including launching a potential hostile takeover of the industrial fund. ING executives in the Netherlands were upset and angry as events spun out of their control.

We could not be aggressive. Investa had virtually no money, and Morgan Stanley was working for ING globally. When things seemed completely stalled, I flew to Amsterdam for a two-hour meeting with senior officials at ING bank and was joined by Chris Niehaus, who flew in from a meeting in London. Chris and I assured ING representatives we were not hostile and were a good and trustworthy partner to deal with. Fortunately, the meeting went very well and negotiations resumed between ING and Investa. It was the longest distance – 25 hours by plane – I have ever gone for a single meeting, but it was essential to put the negotiations back on track.

As our discussions continued, the ING point person, Christophe Tanghe, often called me from the Netherlands in his morning, which was my night. Calls typically started at 9:30 p.m. and often lasted late into the night. Christophe liked to talk. When we finished, I would type up my notes and send them out by email. I did not get much sleep during the long period of negotiations.

Christophe was an interesting character. He was from Belgium, but had developed a streak of stubbornness that I associate more with his Dutch colleagues. He was very tall and extremely handsome with an outdoor weathered look; I often thought Christophe should be a ski instructor – maybe he was in an earlier life. Often my discussions with Christophe would hit an impasse, and he would react with emotion and passion; in those cases I knew to back off and seek another route to address the same issue.

One Saturday afternoon my mobile phone rang while I was walking through Hyde Park in Sydney. It was Christophe.

"Scott, we do not like Macquarie advising both you and Goodman. The two deals are taking different tracks. We are happy to continue to work with you, but only if you hire Morgan Stanley as investment advisors."

I responded in disbelief, "Christophe, how can we hire Morgan Stanley? They are your advisors."

He had anticipated my response and replied quickly, "Not in Australia."

"So you want me to hire the same advisors you are using but just not in Australia?" I asked. "Morgan Stanley would be conflicted. They would not be able to take on the assignment. ING would have to waive the conflict. Christophe, this is messy."

"Scott, we have already waived the conflict. You should call Morgan Stanley and make the offer," Christophe said.

So I hired Morgan Stanley but kept Macquarie in the background for its advice. I was told I could only talk to the Morgan Stanley investment bankers in Australia and not anywhere else because of the potential conflict in interest.

At one point I was so frustrated with ING's constantly changing negotiations, I called the senior Morgan Stanley banker in Europe, whom I knew, and left a message: "I know I cannot talk to you so I am just leaving a message. The ING guys are driving me crazy. Who makes decisions there? Can I trust their point person?"

The subsequent answers were "Bill Connelly makes the decisions and is an honest guy. The other guy is a consultant who is serving as their point person in your deal. He does not have the same reputation as the ING executives."

Later, I met with an outside advisor for the ING board of directors in Sydney and asked if I could trust what the ING representatives were telling me. The answer was not reassuring. Negotiations were sufficiently difficult but when it was clear I could not rely on what the seller's representatives were telling me, it became even more arduous.

As the deal progressed, I became increasing frustrated by ING's constantly changing positions. By all accounts, Bill Connelly was a trustworthy, straightforward guy, but there were layers of people between him and me who had a variety of agendas. And Bill was in Amsterdam, which is the other side of the world. If we were to get a deal done, I had to work things out between all the disparate interests closer to home.

With Goodman buying IIF stock and threatening ING with a hostile takeover, Macquarie advised us to start accumulating stock in IOF, thereby applying pressure on ING. The only problem was that we had no money. We opened a brokerage account with Macquarie and proceeded to buy $100,000 of stock instead of the $100 million they recommended as a minimum. IOF had a market capitalization of about $1.8 billion, so $100,000 was completely insignificant. I just wanted to be able to say we were buying stock if anyone asked. Macquarie never heard of someone buying such a little stake in a mergers-and-acquisitions contest, but the more they thought about the tactic, the more they liked the idea. Doing something that made no obvious sense would cause great concern at ING, they reasoned. ING would assume we would not just buy $100,000, so we must be accumulating a bigger stake using a synthetic structure to mask our purchases. There would be no other logical explanation in their view.

In a later meeting with the ING board of directors, Christophe Tanghe asked me pointedly if we were accumulating stock, which would be viewed as a threatening action. I confirmed we had purchased IOF stock but declined to indicate how much.

Jonathan, Ming, and Campbell stifled their desire to break into open laughter. ING and the board assumed we were buying a major stake in the stock and were considering going hostile. They had no idea we were virtually broke. I do believe it moved the deal forward because of their fear that we had joined with Goodman in considering a hostile undertaking, and had begun accumulating a significant stake in IOF.

About the same time, local journalists began to speculate on who would take over the ING funds. It was clear Goodman intended to acquire the industrial fund and there began to be considerable speculation that Investa was going after the ING Office fund. One article even suggested Investa was "cashed up" and ready to pounce. We had a good laugh about that.

We had frequent meetings and negotiating sessions with the ING staff in Sydney and most were unproductive. I recall one important meeting that was scheduled to start at 5 p.m. at ING's office. Earlier, I had agreed to participate in a sailboat regatta the same day as part of the Property Industry Foundation, which Investa supports. Our boat captain assured me we would be back two hours before my meeting, but well into the race the wind died and we made very slow progress. I was becoming increasingly nervous.

"Skipper," I said, "we need to be back at the marina no later than 4 p.m. This is really important," I said. I was the CEO and we did charter the boat so I thought I had some influence.

"We cannot make the wind blow," he replied.

"Then we need to skip some buoys and shortcut the race," I replied.

"Can't do that. No worries; I promise to have you back in time."

We arrived back after 5 p.m., and I was an hour late for our meeting. I had neglected to realize that the boat race was more important to the skipper than my meeting. Once again, I was reminded of the importance of understanding everyone's needs and priorities in any discussion or negotiation.

As we analyzed the data on IOF that ING made available, it was clear that its books and records were in terrible shape. I complained in an email to Christophe Tanghe and questioned whether ING had liability for such poor accounting practices. He forwarded my email to the other directors, and their negative reaction threatened to derail the deal completely. After a few days of not talking, we managed to patch things up and resumed the negotiations.

After considerable debate and negotiation, ING finally agreed to sell us the management platform for IOF for $20 million. The annual management fees were $8.6 million, so the deal was incredibly attractive and profitable. Normally, management companies trade at about 1.5 to 2 percent of funds under management. We were buying for less than 1 percent, so the price was very attractive.

ING also agreed to not require us to buy the remaining problem plagued "orphan funds" because of the representations and warranties we insisted upon. This was a considerable concession to us and made the deal even more appealing.

MSREF had recovered from the bleak days of 2008 and 2009 but were still constrained by how much capital they could access. The MSREF Investment Committee scraped up $60 million, including $20 million to buy the management platform, and almost $40 million to buy ING's stock in IOF, which Ming promptly pledged as security for a different loan. Denis Hickey, CEO of ING in Sydney, called me and asked if we could close a few days early because news of the acquisition had leaked out. We had not received the money wired from Morgan Stanley yet so I had to decline. I do not think anyone in Australia realized we were running a multi-billion dollar company with such a minimal working cash balance.

The purchase of IOF was a great buy. It reinvigorated staff after years of belt-tightening, asset sales, and retrenchments. It was a moment of sunshine in a still-cloudy economic environment. After reducing our staff from a peak of 680 to a low of 240, we actually hired new people, including ING employees, to join us.

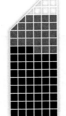

Chapter 18

CORPORATE TURNAROUNDS AMID THE SUNSHINE OF SAN DIEGO

I joined Investa in 2008 because of my long-term relationship with Morgan Stanley and MSREF executives' familiarity with my track record of turning around poorly performing companies. This record and experience began with an unexpected phone call.

Early in 1983 when I was working for Barton-Aschman in Evanston, I received a call from the Hahn Company in San Diego. Hahn was a prestigious shopping mall developer and owner and was looking for someone to start up a market research and financial valuation department. I met with Vernon Schwartz, the CFO, and then John Gilchrist, the CEO, and was consequently offered a job with a salary much higher than I was making at Barton-Aschman in Evanston. However, I needed to convince Jill to move to San Diego. She had stopped working but had made friends and enjoyed our life in Evanston.

She flew to San Diego and stayed with her cousins, Joann and Eric Weitzen, and immediately liked the town. She found a house with a pool and a view and made an offer to buy it. We moved in the summer of 1983 and lived in San Diego until 1995.

I joined the Hahn Company as vice president of Market Research and was very involved in financial modeling as well as market feasibility studies for new developments. Eventually, I became senior vice president for Corporate Development, which included acquisitions, new developments, research, and financial analyses.

A couple of months after joining Hahn, I received a call from Harold Milavsky, whom I had never heard of. Harold told me he needed a detailed financial analysis of every property Hahn owned, including future cash flow projections. He told me to provide a proposal within a week specifying what it would take to complete the task in three months.

At the time, Hahn had no financial projections. We didn't even own personal computers. We had a big mainframe, programmed in COBOL language, which was used for accounting. No one had ever done a cash flow report for the company.

I approached Hahn's CFO, Vernon Schwartz, and asked who the hell Harold Milavsky was. He said Harold was CEO of Trizec, which owned the Hahn Company, and told me to give Harold anything and everything he wanted. So I drew up a proposal to spend $200,000 buying personal computers with budget and valuations software and hiring staff to input and test data. Then I requested additional staff to be reassigned within Hahn and laid out a plan to accomplish "mission: impossible." Vernon talked to Harold and then gave me the go-ahead.

No one expected me to succeed given the state of information at Hahn, but no one wanted to be blamed for the failure because they refused to approve my requests for money and staff. It was my show to succeed or fail, and no one else was betting on success. Harold Milavsky, incidentally, had the reputation of a tough taskmaster who was never satisfied.

My staff and I, including Bill Speer and Kirill Donnelly, worked round the clock for three months and turned out detailed financial reports on every mall (about 45) we owned including graphs, charts, and cash flows. Harold and Kevin Benson, the president of Trizec, flew down for the presentation and were totally impressed.

A month later, Harold called to inform me I was needed to work on a Trizec task force evaluating a potential corporate takeover target. John Gilchrest, Hahn's CEO, objected because he wanted me to focus on Hahn projects, which is why I was hired. Harold dismissed John's complaints, and I spent the next couple of months visiting and analyzing Bramalea's extensive portfolio of offices, housing projects, and retail centers throughout the U.S.

Near the end of the process, I would fly into a city, meet with Harold and his staff beginning around midnight, and brief them on Bramalea's operations in that particular city. The next day, Ken Fields, the CEO of Bramalea, would make a presentation on local operations, but because of my research and late-night briefings, the Trizec guys were well prepared to probe into the details.

One morning at breakfast, Harold asked me to join him, Ken Fields, and Gordon Arnell, Trizec's executive vice president and later the CEO of Brookfield Properties. During breakfast, Harold looked at Ken and said, "Scott told me the information on this portfolio is not what you told me. Either you or he is lying. Which one of you is lying?" I was stunned. Ken Fields had about $100 million in the bank and was CEO of a big company; I was a research guy in my mid 30s just trying to pay our monthly bills. Harold knew I was right and was baiting Ken. He wanted to make sure Ken did not overestimate his company's performance in the future. But it was an uncomfortable moment for me early in my career.

Trizec was a Canadian company that was controlled by the Bronfman Family (Brascan) and the Reichmann family (Olympia & York). Trizec was in financial trouble by the early 1990s due partly to subsequent land acquisitions by Bramalea, which did not work out, and troubles at Olympia & York (Canary Wharf and other issues). Trizec began to pull money out of Hahn to support its financial requirements in Canada. Soon we were all highly leveraged and struggling with the burden of high levels of debt and economic recession.

After dinner on a Thursday night in Manhattan, I walked back to the hotel with Joe Kiely, the CFO of Trizec. Joe asked, "Scott, have you ever been to Holland, Michigan?"

"Actually, Joe, I have. My sister lives in nearby North Muskegon, and it is not too far from where I grew up in Chicago."

Joe continued, "Scott, you should make plans to go there soon and look at the shopping center Bramalea owns in Holland."

"Sure," I replied. "What's the timetable?"

"Tomorrow," he said.

"Tomorrow?" I responded with surprise.

"Yes, why don't you plan to go there tomorrow and then call me Monday with how much the property is worth."

"Joe," I continued, "I assume this is really important?"

"Yes," he replied.

"Okay, Holland, Michigan, here I come."

After a quick visit to Holland that Friday and working over the weekend to review budgets for the center and financial forecasts, I called Joe on Monday.

"Joe, I have not had much time, but my guess is the property is probably worth $30-$35 million. It is a nice mall but very small and relatively isolated from major population centers."

"Thanks, Scott. Let's pay $34 million. Hahn will buy the property and close this Friday, before 2 p.m. Would you please have the paperwork and legalities taken care of?"

"Joe, I don't understand. You want us to buy a regional shopping mall in a week with no due diligence and no more analysis than what I did at home over the weekend, and you want us to close this week? Normally the process takes three to four months."

"Scott, just close the deal Friday before 2 p.m."

Evidently, Bramalea had a payroll run at 2 p.m. that Friday, and Trizec did not want it to miss the payments, which would almost certainly have brought down the company, but they also wanted to make sure the price was fair. We worked day and night and closed the deal in record time.

Steve Bowers, who was responsible for acquisitions for Hahn, actually had that week off. When he returned, he asked if he missed anything. He was more than surprised when we told him we bought and closed on a regional mall the week he was on holiday.

At the same time Hahn's debt levels were rising, the company's development pipeline slowed in response to a general market slowdown. The company struggled with high overhead expenses and a mixed portfolio of shopping malls, ranging from very high-quality fashion malls to second-tier smaller malls that were losing money. The national economy dipped into recession.

Trizec hired Bain & Company (Bain) to recommend how best to proceed and hopefully survive; they asked me to be the primary Hahn contact with the Bain team. In the midst of Bain's work, I felt one solution was to split the Hahn Company into two companies: a very profitable fashion mall company and a lower quality, money-losing second-tier mall company. I did not feel the Hahn Company would survive without making major changes, including reducing high operating costs, and I further believed the lesser quality properties could perform better if given proper focus and effort. I volunteered to be CEO of the "bad bank," which was subsequently named Plaza Properties of America (PPA). The name was selected, incidentally, because our offices were in the Plaza building complex in San Diego.

The Bain team, led by Greg Brenneman, endorsed the plan, and Trizec approved it over the Hahn Company CEO's objections. PPA was created. I was able to recruit several talented colleagues from Hahn to join me at PPA despite the poor quality of our portfolio and the obvious challenges. Some of the remaining Hahn executives, especially the CFO, were critical of those who moved to PPA, leaving the safety of the big company for the "opportunity" to manage and redevelop unwanted, money-losing properties.

We were determined to create a new operating model that drew upon our local presence and innovation. It was unprecedented within the industry at the time.

We encouraged locally based decision-making. On-site property managers were tasked with making key operating decisions and budgetary allocations. They were on site and knew best what the properties needed. We empowered them to use their local knowledge to find local tenants and create marketing programs tailored to local needs and preferences, in contrast to centrally controlled management.

While empowering local managers, we maintained strict financial controls at corporate offices to ensure budgetary discipline and cost containment.

Every key issue in the company was subject to team-based problem solving. Any problem was everybody's problem. Even our assistants had a voice in how to tackle difficult issues. The corporate open office layout also encouraged interaction, which was important. Bonuses were a blend of individual achievements and team performance, so everyone was incentivized to work together to create solutions.

Creativity and innovative solutions were encouraged. In vacant spaces, when none of the traditional retail anchors would lease space, we sought local tenants and non-traditional space users such as governmental offices.

Intensive focus, accountability, and open communications drove the business culture. Some of these principals were learned long ago in the factory in Cicero, Illinois, and others were based on observations in other assignments. I do believe everyone knows something I do not know, which can be helpful in solving problems. And everyone has a voice and wants to be heard. Listen and you will earn the loyalty and work commitment otherwise not possible.

With an aligned and motivated staff and organization, we began to focus on our challenging portfolio of properties. I recall driving from Colorado Springs to Pueblo, Colorado, where we owned a mall. On the drive, I noticed signs advertising land for sale at $20 per acre. Clearly, there was not much demand for property in the area. Driving into Pueblo, I saw an innovative landscaping plan for the first time. Several houses in the neighborhood near the mall had paved over the grass in their front yards with concrete or asphalt. They then parked their cars more conveniently next to the front doors. Pueblo was not an affluent town, and we began immediately to change the merchandize and tenant mix within the mall accordingly. The new tenants may not have been suitable for the Hahn fashion malls, but they were just fine for Pueblo, Colorado.

Another time I met with our on-site staff in Barstow, California. Barstow is well known because it is about midway between Los Angeles and Las Vegas on Interstate 10. Unfortunately, not many people lived in this dessert community, and we owned a mall there. In addition to our mall, three developers had built off-price malls, so the area had almost no people and lots of retail shops.

I asked the staff if the mall ever had a busy day. "Sure," they replied. "Whenever there is a big accident on I-10 and the highway is closed, people stop in Barstow to get out of the intense heat and wait for the highway to clear." So our fate was to be determined by how many times a year the highway was closed. Eventually, we sold the mall to the city, which converted it to a city hall; this was a good outcome for everyone.

One of our biggest challenges was our mall in Ogden, Utah. It was located in downtown Ogden, north of Salt Lake City. The City was not growing or particularly well known. I thought the key to saving the mall was to add destination attractions, attracting customers from suburban areas. I tried to recruit ZCMI, a Utah department store then controlled by the Mormon Church to relocate its freestanding store into the mall, but I was unsuccessful. We did add a kinetic sculpture to its center court, and people did watch the balls fall through a series of moving obstacles on their way from top to bottom. Customers were mesmerized, but we needed more shopping destinations.

Finally, I had an inspiration. I called Alan Collier, a friend and real estate guy in Utah, who was also active in the Mormon Church.

"Alan, there is a Mormon temple next to our mall in Ogden. How did it get there? Is it active; does it need more space? Do they want to buy the mall and expand?"

"Scott, nice try, but the temple is too big already and was never supposed to be built there. The reason it was built on that site is the church bought some land in the mountains for a new temple but one of the church elders had an inspiration from God, who told him the temple should be in downtown Ogden and not in the mountains. We take such messages seriously."

"So, Alan, if God thought it was so important for the temple to be built in downtown Ogden, what would God think if the mall became derelict, causing a blight on his temple and downtown?"

"Scott, where are you going with this?"

"Just connecting dots. I think the church should arrange for ZCMI to relocate to the mall and would ask those who know more about this stuff to reason whether this was part of God's plan. I have no such expertise."

"I will set up a meeting for you to make a presentation to the decision makers, but you must not suggest you are in a position to interpret God's wishes. This is something for the church to consider internally."

"Will you raise the issue?"

"I will consider it, but I need to think about it and discuss it with some others."

A month later with Alan's help and presence, I made a presentation on why ZCMI should be in the mall. I showed the site plans and always included the temple to remind everyone of the proximity, but never mentioned God. Aside from the religious connection, Alan and I believed the relocation of a department store from a free standing older site into the mall made good commercial sense for ZCMI. After a few questions, they asked me to leave. Alan left a few minutes later and joined me outside.

"Alan, what just happened?"

"They will move ZCMI into the mall. You had better do a good job fixing up the mall; the audience is bigger than you think."

On one of my many visits to Utah, I was asleep late at night in a hotel in Salt Lake City when the hotel phone rang, jarring me awake.

"Hello," I answered sleepily.

"Scott, it's Alan. We are in the hotel bar. There are some people here you need to meet. You need to get down here as soon as possible."

I showed up in the pub 10 minutes later.

"Alan, I didn't think you guys drank."

"We drink, just not alcohol." So we toasted non-alcoholic cocktails well after midnight and talked about Ogden City.

PPA renovated the mall and added a new ZCMI store, which provided a destination and activated the mall. The mall was successful for a time when PPA owned and operated it, but subsequently Dillard's department store joined with an out-of-town developer to create another suburban mall in competition. The May Company bought ZCMI and relocated it into the suburban mall, securing the downtown mall's fate.

With motivated staff, empowered local managers, and an intense focus on our assets, PPA began to perform almost immediately. In the first year, operating cash flow moved from a loss of $5 million to profitability. The assets received far more attention than they did when bundled with bigger, more glamorous fashion malls. Meanwhile, the Hahn Company continued to limp along with high debt, over-staffing, management silos, and bloated expenses.

After about two years at PPA, the Trizec CEO terminated Hahn's senior management and asked me to rejoin Hahn as acting CEO to fix the big company, utilizing lessons learned at PPA. The "bad bank" was actually outperforming the "good bank" by then in budgetary performance measures and growth.

At Hahn, I terminated one-third of the corporate staff and implemented similar programs that were tested and successful at PPA. This was my second corporate restructuring in two years. I met personally with every employee who was retrenched; it was a very difficult and stressful time for me.

Morgan Stanley was watching my efforts with interest. In 1994

MSREF bought a Houston, Texas-based shopping center company, which was struggling and in need of a turnaround. Chris Niehaus began calling and asking me to consider leaving Hahn and taking the reins at Center America Property Trust (CAPT).

Then Trizec failed and was taken over by another company led by Peter Monk and Jerry O'Conner. Jerry wanted his own guy running Hahn and hired Lee Wagman, whom he knew through industry committees but had never worked with. I was informed that Lee would be the new CEO of Trizec Hahn, and I was asked to stay on as COO. I met Lee and decided he and I were very different, and I did not feel comfortable working with him. I was also physically and mentally worn out by the intense work level and stress of retrenchments and reorganization. I accepted the MSREF offer to take over its struggling platform and moved my family to Houston in August 1995.

While busy at work and dealing with so many issues at Hahn and Trizec, the period spent in San Diego was a terrific time for our family lives. Ross, our second son, was born in February 1986, which was the second happiest moment of my life. Jill and I went to see the movie *Out of Africa* and her water broke when we returned home. We dropped Andrew off at a neighbor's house, and proceeded to Sharp Hospital. Like Andrew, Ross was not ready to be delivered, and we walked the floors of the hospital much of the night. Ross was born in the morning.

Andrew and Ross spent their formative years in San Diego. I coached their Little League baseball teams each year, and Jill and I coached Ross's soccer team one year. Andrew and I went to the San Diego Zoo together almost every Saturday morning. We rode the merry-go-round outside the entrance, ate ice cream, and wandered about, looking at the animals. Both Andrew and Ross took classes at the zoo on weekends; we had such fun hanging out. My fondest memories were time spent with my sons as they were growing up.

I took Andrew to school or to the school bus when he was in junior high school, which allowed Jill to stay home with Ross. On special occasions, I would drive Andrew to Solana Beach, we would have a cinnamon bun together at a small bakery, and then I would drop him at school nearby. Sometimes, he asked me to drop him off a block from the bus stop because it was "uncool" to be seen with a parent at that time; I understood.

Coaching Andrew's and then Ross's Little League baseball teams was an important priority with me despite work pressures at Hahn. A few years ago, I had dinner in London with Carla Giannini, a senior investment banker who worked on a deal with me many years ago when I lived in San Diego. She recalled the time when we had a dozen high-powered attorneys, investment bankers, and investment fund representatives on the line for a conference call regarding a big deal. I told everyone at the start of the call that I had a conflict beginning at 3 p.m. and would have to end the call at that time. When 3 p.m. arrived and the call was not nearly over, I announced the call had to end regardless because I was leaving. The unanimous response was for me to postpone my other meeting; the conference call was too important to end prematurely. I replied that I had Little League practice at 3:30 and was responsible for a dozen little kids who would not wait for attorneys to finish their debate. The phone line went silent; all were in disbelief. But I ended the call and went to Little League.

Carla is the second investment banker to recall the memory of that story long after it occurred, and to tell me how much respect she had for someone willing to put family commitments ahead of business needs because it was so uncommon. Eventually, we did finalize the deal, and our Little League team went on to a successful season.

When Andrew turned 12 years old, I was asked to coach an advanced or "major" league team. I told the league president I would do so if Andrew qualified for the Major Leagues at spring tryouts.

"But if you agree to coach, Andrew automatically qualifies," the president told me.

"No," I replied. "The only way I will coach is if Andrew earns a spot through his own performance. Andrew has earned whatever he has accomplished, and he would not feel right if he were invited to play in the Majors only because his Dad was a coach."

The league president was surprised because most parents tried to use their influence to benefit their sons, but he agreed. At spring tryouts, Andrew had a stellar performance and easily qualified with no help from me.

Years later, Ross applied for admission to Davidson College, which was very selective and difficult to gain admission. He badly wanted to go to Davidson but also wanted to know he earned the right to go due to his own efforts. He specifically asked me not to talk to anyone at Davidson on his behalf. I had made some donations to Davidson when Andrew was a student there, but I honored Ross's request. Ross earned his admission just as Andrew had.

We acquired our third child while in San Diego. He had four legs and was named Nanuk by a former owner. Ross was 8 years old and Andrew 13. It was an overcast day in San Diego and gloomy even in Rancho Santa Fe, which lies inland from the coast. Jill was out of town, visiting her mother, as I recall. Andrew had a soccer game in Rancho Santa Fe, and Ross and I were there to cheer him on. Ross's soccer game started a couple hours after Andrew's finished, and we boys had time to kill.

Across the street from the Rancho Santa Fe soccer field was Helen Woodward Animal Center, a care-and-adoption facility for pets, especially dogs. With time on our hands and nothing better to do, we wandered across the street to the facility. This was a fateful journey.

I had grown up with a dog. Mandy was my best friend as a child. She watched over me when I was only crawling, and went everywhere with me when I was walking. I know the attachment that can form between a boy and his dog.

Andrew and Ross were immediately enthused about the idea of adopting a dog. As we wandered through the outdoor pens, Andrew was attracted to Charlie, one of the most enthusiastic and excited dogs in the place. Ross was attracted to a shy but comely dog that looked part-golden retriever and part-something else. I was concerned the shy dog would not be as friendly if adopted. I was wrong.

When Jill returned, two bubbling boys, who could not wait to share their excitement about what they saw at Helen Woodward, confronted her. It was not fair. Jill had never spent much time around dogs and was definitely not a fan of owning one. But no one could resist the excitement that poured from the two boys with ever more promises of taking care of the pet. Her resistance melted under the earnest pleadings of her young sons.

Upon returning to Helen Woodward, Jill did not care for Charlie. That was okay, because another family was there and wanted to adopt the nonstop jumping and gyrating Charlie. A single, working woman, who wanted to adopt Nanuk, was viewing him. Jill liked the shy dog's looks and demeanor, and the Helen Woodward staff could not resist Ross's imploring that Nanuk be given a home with a family instead of a single person. We left that day with Nanuk.

It did not take Nanuk long to adopt his new family. He had lived with a woman for four years and then had been given up for adoption when she lost a place to keep him during the day when she was at work. Nanuk was not shy; he had been rejected by the only person he was ever attached to and put in a sterile pen. He was depressed and probably feared added rejection. Once he realized we would not reject him, he moved right into the family circle.

Nanuk's biggest failing was his desire to be everyone's friend. A couple of times on evening walks in San Diego, Nanuk encountered a skunk and ran up to the furry black-and-white creature with tail wagging and a clear desire to play. I recall taking a very smelly dog home one night, and Andrew and I washing him with Campbell's tomato soup, because I read that tomato sauce helped mitigate the skunk smell. It didn't work very well, but Nanuk did not seem fussed about his new odor and enjoyed licking the soup.

In San Diego I was held up one more time. I was at the neighborhood shopping center in Carmel Valley and had just taken some cash out of the Bank of America ATM. It was a Saturday afternoon on a typical sunny San Diego summer day. A teenager with a slight build approached me and showed what looked like the handle to a gun in his gym bag and demanded my wallet. I had learned from Washington, D.C., professionals, and was not about to give up my wallet without verification of a real and loaded gun. I lectured the kid on what trouble he would be in if he pursued this line of inquiry. The would-be assailant became a bit agitated and pulled the gun from his bag and pointed it at me. I asked if he needed the wallet, or if cash would be sufficient. He was really becoming upset and grabbed the wallet and ran. There were so many witnesses by then, that he was later apprehended by the police with my wallet and his gun. The police gave me a really hard time about trying to negotiate with a gunman, but it worked out okay.

I continued my long-distance running when I was in San Diego. My running, which started when I sought to rebuild my knee after the Marines, was my refuge from stress and pressure throughout my work career. In San Diego I ran at lunchtime, usually with Mike Heiken, the Hahn controller. Mike and I often talked about accounting and finance issues, and I learned much of what I know about accounting and financial reporting from the many hours of discussion with Mike as we ran through the campus of the University of California in San Diego every week. I ran in a couple half marathons in San Diego, but my knee was never strong enough to survive training for marathons.

San Diego was a very nice chapter in our family life. Andrew graduated from junior high school and Ross finished third grade in San Diego. Jill served as president of the school board, and Nanuk befriended everyone he met. But conditions always change and nothing lasts forever. In life and in business, change is continuous and nonstop until life itself stops.

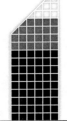

Chapter 19

REFINANCING A $3 BILLION LOAN WHEN BANKS DON'T WANT TO LEND

The "trick play" brought us another year without a loan default, but Investa still had the big Hold Portfolio loan with an approaching maturity date. MSREF had borrowed $3 billion against a portfolio of our office buildings. We had reduced the loan balance with the trick play to about $2.7 billion. The LTV was about 82 percent. We knew the most we could hope for on refinancing was about 60 percent LTV. So we had to pay the balance down by at least $700 million. We could not rely on Morgan Stanley; the company had survived but was still constrained for cash. We had to sell assets in a difficult market.

We worked through a scenario of what had to happen for us to raise the capital and close the gap between existing loan balance and what we thought we could borrow in a new loan facility. A series of tasks was required to be successfully concluded, one after another. My assistant, Elpie Vanos, equated the challenge to a game of dominoes and even drew up a picture of dominoes listing each task.

We had to sell several big assets for cash, and there were few buyers capable of buying such a large supply. Our strategy was to sell assets to related partners at prices they found attractive and would withstand investor scrutiny. This included having our partner buy a portion of our interest in the Grosvenor office building in Sydney. It also included ICPF buying three buildings from us, but before they could, they needed to raise about $350 million of new capital, secure approval from their independent board of directors, and secure further approval in a vote of the investors, because this would be a "related-party" deal.

IOF was to buy two assets from us but before they could, they had to sell their portfolio of U.S. office buildings and repatriate the funds to Australia. Then the company needed to secure approval from their independent board members and approval in a vote of the shareholders, because of the related-party nature of the transaction.

We needed property valuations on the remaining assets to increase by almost 9 percent and confirmed by independent valuers. Then we still had to secure bank commitments for almost $2 billion for the remaining portfolio of assets.

The game of Investa dominoes commenced, and the outcome determined if we survived. Each domino had to fall as planned, or we would not succeed.

The IOF fund manager and I flew to the U.S. and met with our advisors, Clarion Partners in New York. I had known the principal there, Steve Furnary, for many years; I needed his help and attention. IOF needed to sell its remaining office buildings there before year-end and bring the proceeds home. This would not be easy.

The IOF building in New York City was really a 49 percent interest in an older B grade building on 3rd Avenue, outside the main office core in Manhattan. The majority partner, an international fund manager, was notorious even by New York standards for being difficult to deal with. No one else was going to buy a 49 percent non-managing and non-controlling interest. The partner was the only logical buyer and we both knew it.

I met with an old friend, who directed U.S. asset management at MSREF. He was responsible for most of MSREF's transactions. When I told him who our partner was, he said we were screwed. MSREF had owned a 49 percent interest in another building with the same partner and had great difficulty selling its interest because of obstructions from the partner. He told me to expect a low price and a closing far into the future. The more I pushed the need to sell, the lower the price the partner would offer.

I also called another old friend, Gene Pinover, a top attorney in New York, and asked Gene to talk to our partner in the deal. Gene worked closely with this fund manager and represented the company in many negotiations. Gene reported back that our partner expected to buy our interest, was in no hurry, and would buy only at a bargain price. We needed to sell quickly at a premium price. Gene's comments were reinforced by the managing partner when we subsequently met in his office.

The second IOF building was in Plano, Texas. It was very dated and was struggling in a sea of suburban Dallas vacancy. The building had not been updated for years; the color scheme was purple and yellow, as I recall. I felt sick when I saw it. It would not be an easy disposition, but we had a good local realtor and Clarion's team was focused.

The third IOF building was an 80 percent interest in a beautiful office building in downtown Washington, D.C. This building was well located and a premium asset. It had too many vacancies, and brokers recommended we wait to sell the building until it was better occupied. We could not wait. I was also nervous that the U.S. federal government was running huge deficits, and if the government ever decided to balance its budget, layoffs in D.C. would potentially devastate the office market.

The even bigger issue with the D.C. office building, however, was that our partner in the investment was also the property manager and leasing agent and had an evergreen management contract. He could not be terminated. Most prospective buyers would not purchase a building if they could not control management.

I flew to Washington and met with the partner, whom I knew from many years ago when I was just starting my career. Chip Akridge and I worked together briefly 40 years before. We had a good time reminiscing, but Chip was not about to help me if it meant losing his management of the prized building. We needed to find a buyer who had a relationship with Chip and was comfortable with not controlling management. Eventually this led to only two possibilities. We just needed one of them to step up.

Eventually we sold the New York building to the partner, but at full price. I hired Eastdil Secured (Eastdil) to represent us and gave them until Christmas to produce an acceptable deal or lose its commission and the listing. Eastdil succeeded in eliciting an acceptable offer with only a few days to spare. I think the company was concerned about its reputation and the prospect of losing the deal to a competitor. Eastdil managed to convince our partner that our offer was pretty good, and we would not sell at a discount.

The Eastdil office in Washington, D.C., managed to secure a bid for the D.C. office building from an Asian buyer who had an existing relationship with Chip Akridge. The bid was at a price that surpassed even our high hopes.

Finally, Clarion and its local broker convinced a Texas-based office developer and owner to buy and redevelop the Plano property. They put together a drawing on how the building could look if refurbished. If a picture is worth a thousand words, the Plano drawings were worth millions of dollars.

The proceeds from the three transactions transferred back to Australia by January 2012, and a critical domino fell.

Michael Cook negotiated an agreement to sell a 5 percent interest in the Grosvenor office building to our partner. We argued about values and pricing but eventually reached a fair deal. This equalized ownership, and another domino fell.

Pete Menegazzo worked tirelessly to raise capital as the fund manager of ICPF. Pete needed to raise about $350 million, which was a very aggressive target. He had raised $200 million in 2010, which was critical for paying down debt, funding operations, and buying assets. At one point, it looked like ICPF was close to reaching the goal, but then one big investor, Funds SA, unexpectedly downsized its commitment. Pete called me when I was in London as part of a trip to visit European investors.

"I just talked to Mark Coleman at Funds SA. With the world markets in turmoil, they cannot give us the $100 million that we thought they had committed. We are short and there is no one else in the wings ready to contribute. Unless we raise debt to undesired levels, we will not get to where we need to be to buy the office building we want."

"Pete," I replied, "I will call Mark when I return to Sydney. He needs to step up for the full amount. He is an honorable guy and if I read him right, he will do it. He committed and he is the type of guy to honor his commitments."

"It is not Mark," Pete replied. "His CIO does not think investing in real estate is the right thing to do right now."

"Stay calm, I will call Mark," I said.

The next week I did call Mark Coleman. Until then, he was recovering from surgery in the hospital and I was not about to call him there. We had a long talk and I reminded him that we were counting on him, and he had given us assurances that if we made certain assets available, he would be there to support us.

The next day, Mark called back and confirmed they would make the full commitment despite reservations on the overall market. I had read Mark correctly. He is a classy guy with an impeccable reputation. One thing I have learned in my career is the importance of picking good partners and business relationships. Another domino fell.

The independent board of ICPF approved the deal after many studies and expert advice. David Baffsky, the chairman, is a tough taskmaster and very independent as are his two fellow board members, Jim Evans and Dennis Wildenburg. They needed to be sure the deal was in the best interests of the investors, and the investors were getting a good deal. David Baffsky and Pete Menegazzo make a formidable negotiating team. The ICPF investors are well served by their independent board. The investors then approved the deal overwhelmingly despite active opposition from one of the investor consultants who was opposed to the use of Macquarie Bank to help in the fundraising. Two more dominoes fell.

It is important to note that all of the "domino deals" we negotiated were essential for Investa's survival, but each deal was also a good deal for the buyers. ICPF and IOF benefited greatly from each and every transaction we entered into. I learned many years ago, a good deal is always a deal in which all the participants "win." I think the investors knew we would be fair and they would benefit from each transaction, and that made the deals easier to accomplish.

With the funds back from the U.S., IOF was cashed up and able to buy. We worked out an agreement with the IOF fund manager to buy two assets from our balance sheet. Again, an independent board needed to approve the deal, and they went through a rigorous process of independent valuations and experts. At one stage, the independent board chairman of IOF, Debbie Page, notified me that its valuer disagreed with the pricing on one of the assets, and we would have to lower the price if we wanted the board to approve the deal. I was convinced the valuer was wrong and we could sell the asset on the open market for more, but we were running out of time. I agreed to reduce the price.

Finally, the IOF deal was submitted to the unit holders for a formal vote. The head of one of the big dedicated real estate funds led a public campaign against the deal, asking voters to reject our offer because it was a related-party deal. The controversy played out in the local newspapers. We met with virtually all of the big investors in the fund and explained why it was a good deal. Ultimately, we prevailed by a vote of 92 percent in favor. I always felt we would win approval; it was a good deal for the unit holders. But I was worried, especially when a large real estate investment fund was so publically opposed. Another domino fell.

We were moving around the domino board as the months passed with each piece falling in line. It was nerve-racking, especially if I stepped back and observed the totality of what was required and the tight timeframes. When we just focused on each domino ahead, it was easier to move forward. I often woke up at night worrying about how we were going to accomplish so many sequential tasks. I found myself asking, "What if just one domino did not fall?"

As we were raising equity, we also needed to raise about $2 billion of debt in a fragile banking market. Everyone was extremely nervous because of liquidity concerns about banks globally. We did not see how we could raise so much money in 2012, with the GFC still fresh in memories, Europe and European banks in great distress, U.S. banks under pressure, and all banks facing capital and regulatory issues. We continued to live on knife's edge.

To complicate matters further, Ming decided she did not want to use an investment banker to help us or to syndicate the deal using a lead bank. She wanted to do something unusual but potentially very beneficial to Investa. She proposed a common-terms deed, which all the banks would agree on. And then she would negotiate bilateral deals with each bank so she could pick and choose the best terms instead of all banks agreeing on the same fees and margins. By keeping the banks from cooperating with each other on fees and charges, Investa would receive better overall pricing and have much more flexibility in the future.

She also wanted to arrange the loans over a three-year maturity ranging from three- to five-year tranches. Having almost $2 billion mature in a single year was too risky, she felt.

So we went to market looking for about $2 billion without help from any outside bank or investment banker, proposing an unusual structure that was very beneficial to us, across three different maturity dates. Also, we wanted the new loan to start several months in the future so we could keep the current loan with its favorable pricing in place until its maturity. This is called a forward-start facility. Both the Morgan Stanley team and I had serious doubts, but we did not want to discourage or second-guess my young CFO.

The plan was to lock up the four Australian banks and then move on to offshore banks. We wanted the four big Australian banks to put up at least $300 million each. ANZ and NAB both were supportive, but there were issues with CBA and Westpac.

Our recent history with CBA had not been good, and it was with considerable trepidation that we entered into the next phase of negotiations. The bank did not support us with the Sale Portfolio loan and almost caused us to default. We remained on good terms with our relationship bankers, Peter Barnes and Gary Moody, who were always available to listen and give advice. We struggled with the property risk guys at CBA, however, one of whom I actually referred to as "Darth Vader."

Ming maintained cordial relations with CBA throughout the GFC. Whenever I was negative, she reminded me that even Darth Vader turned out okay in the movie. I give her credit for maintaining the relationship; I also give Peter Barnes, Gary Moody, and their staff credit for maintaining dialogue during very difficult times.

The CBA participation was resolved at a meeting in our boardroom. The CBA team, including the risk officer I referred to as "Darth Vader," came. He was clearly irritated being there; he flipped through papers as if distracted and disinterested.

I began the presentation and talked through the journey we had been on. I reminded the bankers that we had never missed a loan payment during the economic downturn, even when our cash flow was negative and we were selling assets just to pay bills. I reminded them that we never asked to modify a loan agreement or give us relief. When we borrowed money, we recognized the obligation to pay it back on the terms we agreed to at the time of the loan. The risk officer began to pay attention. Then Ming walked through the proposal to refinance the Hold loan. Finally, we asked for questions.

After a moment of silence, he asked what Ming expected of CBA.

"Three-hundred million, which is what we are asking if you want to be a cornerstone bank."

He replied with a hint of sarcasm, "Why would you even think we would consider a $300 million participation?"

Ming replied directly and then I added, the other Australian banks have already made it clear they intended to participate fully.

He asked, "How much are the other banks putting in?"

I replied, "One is already in at $450 million."

He turned to the CBA team and asked them, "If the others are putting in $450 million, why are we not putting in the same amount?"

Everyone was speechless. It was like the real Darth Vader deciding to support the Rebel Fleet.

The next day, CBA's Gary Moody called Ming to say they were proposing a $450 million participation to the bank's credit committee. The entire amount was subsequently approved, and CBA became a key cornerstone in our loan facility.

Westpac was another story. That bank also had been very difficult with us. It had classified us as an at-risk borrower and assigned us to the work-out section in the bank. We usually call it the "bad bank." As a result, we had trouble getting any cooperation, despite our flawless record of paying interest, and never defaulting on a loan or asking for a concession.

Around this time, I was invited to a property luncheon at Westpac hosted by Gail Kelly, CEO, and Rob Whitfield, head of institutional banking. Gail and Rob talked about how Westpac appreciated its customers and was a relationship bank. My experience suggested otherwise. They said they wanted feedback from their customers and were open to suggestions at any time.

When I was leaving the luncheon, Gail and Rob were shaking hands with the departing attendees. I thanked them both for lunch but told them I did not consider Westpac a relationship bank and would be happy to give them feedback if they were really interested. I think they were a bit taken aback at the unexpected comment.

A couple weeks later, a Westpac banker called to set up a meeting for Ming and me with Rob Whitfield at Westpac's corporate headquarters on Kent Street in downtown Sydney. At that meeting, we explained to Rob the issues we had with Westpac, and the history of difficulties. Rob had been well prepared and was familiar with Investa and our relationship with Westpac. I was impressed that someone so high in the bank would be as knowledgeable about the details as was Rob. Late in the meeting, Rob asked, "So what do we need to do to rebuild our relationship with Investa?"

I replied, "Rob, meeting with us and engaging with us is a big step forward. I understand you plan to participate in the Hold refinance, but the bank wants to be involved with setting the terms of the deal and yet is not willing to commit to the minimum $300 million cornerstone threshold. If you want to be a relationship bank and cornerstone the Hold deal, you need to increase your participation from $100 million to $300 million."

I think Ming was surprised how aggressive I appeared. We needed their participation, and it would have created major problems if they passed.

The next week, Stuart Brown of Westpac called Ming and informed her they were putting a request for $300 million to credit for approval. Subsequently, Westpac approved the full amount and became a cornerstone bank to Investa.

By fall, Ming had lined up $1.55 billion from the four Australian cornerstone banks. A major French bank stepped up for $100 million and a major Chinese bank for $150 million, which was its largest property loan to date in Australia. Ming had been courting Bank of China for a couple years and often set up lunches at local Chinese restaurants. Campbell, Jonathan, and I all dreaded going and eating a variety of unusual food. Ming is of Malaysian descent and seemed to enjoy the cuisine. We all enjoyed the company and conversation, just not the food.

We needed $100 million more to reach our revised target level of $1.9 billion, which was the maximum loan amount supportable by the remaining asset pool. We thought a major bank from Germany was there with $200 million, but it came through very late with a series of requirements that other banks did not need. A United Kingdom bank wanted in the deal, but it took the principals longer to gain approvals from England. Finally, they came through for $100 million, and we told the German bank and one other lender we did not need their funds with the extra requirements. Except for finalizing documents, we were done in May 2012.

Like so many other challenges, almost no one thought we would succeed. Raising $1.9 billion in the midst of fears of European collapse, pressures on Greece, Spain, Italy, and others, increased regulatory pressure on all banks, and slowing property markets in Australia was another miracle performance.

I sent our board of directors an email confirming the bank deal was done. It was evidently forwarded throughout Morgan Stanley, because I received many congratulatory emails, including several from people I had not sent the original email to.

I also requested and received board approval to pay our employees a one-time $5,000 bonus each, excluding highly paid executives like me. The collective work of so many Investa employees who worked tirelessly through the GFC keeping the properties fully occupied and controlling costs when we were struggling finally paid off, and I wanted to thank them. The same week they all received their bonus, two competitors announced major retrenchments. The newspapers covered the retrenchments but were uninterested in the special thank-you bonus that Investa's employees received.

I learned long ago that taking care of employees generally results in better corporate results; if you take care of employees, they will take care of you. Buying donuts and making coffee for the typing pool when I was a new associate at Gladstone resulted from the same attitude as paying Investa employees a special bonus 40 years later.

Chapter 20

CENTER AMERICA
PROPERTY TRUST: NO GUNS
IN THE OFFICE, PLEASE

Fixing companies often requires moving to new places and experiencing cultures that are new and outside one's comfort zone. Moving to Sydney was probably easier than moving my family from San Diego to Houston in 1995.

It was characteristically hot and humid in Houston, Texas, in August 1995, but it was not the climate that created problems that day. My first day at Center America (CA) was shocking. I met Mike Foster, the Morgan Stanley executive charged with overseeing the CA investment at a nearby hotel and we drove together to CA's offices. A meeting with the CA executive staff commenced shortly after we arrived.

At the time, this was MSREF's single largest investment since entering the funds business, and the firm's first major investment in an operating company. Its success would greatly influence Morgan Stanley's reputation in the funds business and its ability to raise future funds. The CA investment was underperforming, but I did not know how bad things were. It did not take long to understand the depth of the problems.

Jeff Moore, the president of CA and son of the founders, handed out board books and began to discuss corporate performance of the past month and year-to-date results. Less than 30 minutes into the presentation, I was confused. The tables and graphs showed the company was only leasing about 50 percent of the space it was budgeted to lease and actual revenues were far behind forecast. I assumed I did not understand something. No one misses a budget by 50 percent.

Jeff explained that I was comparing results with "acquisition numbers," which the employees viewed as nonsense. I was stunned. No one at Morgan Stanley had suggested the performance was so far off the forecast. I was familiar with Morgan Stanley and had used them as advisors and bankers in the past, and missing projections, especially by a substantial margin, was not normal for them.

I was confronted with a company that was undercapitalized, losing cash at an alarming rate, and performing badly. When I subsequently visited all 100 of the shopping centers owned, it was clear we were a slum landlord as well, with deteriorating retail shops often located in low-income neighborhoods. I had moved my family from the beaches of San Diego to the heat and humidity of Houston so I could run a money-losing operation of derelict shopping centers. It was shocking and depressing, but I had no alternative but to focus on the challenge before me.

Early during my tenure, a few operational items needed to be dealt with quickly. I banned smoking and guns in the office. In Texas, residents have the right, by law, to carry firearms with a permit unless a policy banning guns was posted. Even the previous CEO carried a gun in her handbag. She pulled it out one night at a restaurant to show Mike Foster and me.

There was a widely told story about a previous meeting in our offices between some New York-based investment bankers and Jerry Moore, Jeff's father. Jerry was showing off a favorite gun, which discharged accidently and sent a bullet past one of the bankers and into the adjacent wall. The bankers departed quickly and never returned.

Jeff Moore, who was often unpredictable, kept a gun in his desk at work. I was unsure how many other employees carried guns, but I did not want to have a disagreement with an employee and learn that he or she was packing a gun.

The day after I banned cigarette smoking and guns, one of the employees stopped by.

"Scott, I understand why you banned smoking in the office because it is bad for our health, but why did you ban guns?"

There were so many legacy issues from when the predecessor company to CA was a family-run business. There were several issues that were generally hidden and not disclosed to Morgan Stanley or other outside parties. For example, an employee asked me before Christmas,

"Scott, are we going to receive blue checks again this year before Christmas?"

"Sorry, but what is a blue check?"

"Every year we receive checks from a different account that we do not have to report to the government."

"No, we will pay bonuses but no blue checks. Sorry."

I had to relocate my office when I realized the conversations in my first office were being listened to. Whenever I talked about Jeff Moore or his sister, who worked there for a time, their mother, Jean, the prior CEO, would be in my office within minutes correcting me or defending the offspring. It was pretty transparent that Jean and Jerry, who owned the office building and had an office there as well, knew exactly what I talked about. After we relocated our office to the second level of a nearby shopping center we owned, we never had an issue again.

In the first couple of years, we changed over 90 percent of the employees and brought in new senior staff to run many of the key functions. Inherited employees had been hired and retained because of family loyalty instead of competence. There were some very competent staff including Mike Axelrad, the corporate attorney, Tex Spear, head of leasing, Glen Havens, who ran our facilities group, and Mike Tones, head of property management. Most of the others needed to be replaced, including the president, Jeff Moore, who was very talented but admitted he preferred a less structured work environment instead of a more corporate, professional environment.

I set up an information technology (IT) department to network our computers and provide contemporary technology, but managing technology guys was always a challenge. One week, the IT director did not show up for work. When he did show the next week, he told me he had been in jail and was only allowed to make one phone call. He chose not to call work. I let him go.

Another IT manager did not get along with his second-in-command. As tensions grew between our two-person IT staff, one informed me the other was taking shortcuts, jeopardizing our system. His colleague, in response, then informed me that the senior manager was running a pornographic website from a computer at his home. I terminated both of them and hired more competent staff with fewer personal agendas.

With intensive focus at CA, we developed plans for each asset and began a process of redevelopment and re-tenanting. I spent much of my time meeting with anchor tenants and rebuilding relationships that had soured under past ownership. Centers that had been starved for capital were rebuilt and repositioned. Facades and roofs were repaired, and improved centers were branded with the new Center America logo. New anchors, including grocery stores and pharmacies, were attracted. Word spread quickly that the new CA team was creating signature neighborhood developments in middle- and low-income neighborhoods.

In addition to redeveloping older centers, we started a new division to leverage our tenant relationships into completely new developments. We expanded outside of Texas and opened an office in Florida that proved very successful.

The team was focused on action and results. Once, we could not obtain approval from a loan trustee to build a pharmacy adjacent to one of our centers, despite its obvious benefit and increase in value to the property. We built it anyway. A year later the trustee called and asked if the pharmacy had always been there; they had just noticed it on an annual visit.

Another time we redeveloped a center and painted it. It looked terrific but the immediately adjacent building, owned by an absentee landlord, looked terrible and detracted from our new image. After trying to contact the owner without success, I told the maintenance crew just to paint the adjacent building at night to match the center. It looked much better and no one ever complained.

We had a center in Brenham, Texas, which badly needed a grocery store anchor, but H-E-B was the only store in town and saw no reason to leave its smaller store and relocate to a bigger facility. With no competition, there was no motivation to upgrade.

Tex Spear hired a helicopter, and we circled the town a few times so it was obvious to everyone in Brenham we were there. Then we landed in our shopping center parking lot, looked around, and took off. The next day, Tex stopped by the H-E-B store in Brenham and mentioned to the manager another grocer was considering locating a big supermarket at our site.

Tex was called soon by the corporate H-E-B guys, concerned about possible competition, and asked to send a new site plan for their evaluation. He did send a plan but with a Kroger store laid out, ostensibly by mistake. H-E-B made the deal to anchor the center with a big new store, thinking they had ensured Kroger would not be able to penetrate the local market without our site. What they did not realize was that Kroger was never interested.

We had one center that was so ugly we could not find any tenants. We decided to tear it down; a vacant lot was more leasable than a dilapidated structure. The center was part of a loan pool with Wells Fargo, so I called the bank representatives and explained we intended to tear down part of its loan security, but the land would be more valuable without the center. They flew a team out from California and approved the demolition. No one could recall a situation where a borrower was permitted to demolish the asset securing a loan without paying off the loan, but we did not have extra cash and the building was actually a liability. Subsequently, we built a beautiful new center on the then-vacant property.

Because many of our centers were located in lower-income neighborhoods, security was often a key issue. If shoppers did not feel safe, they shopped less, and if employees did not feel safe, we lost tenants. One of the tactics we used was to negotiate deals with the local police or sheriff departments to operate a storefront station in higher-risk centers. This usually had the desirable effect of deterring criminals from visiting our properties.

However, even the best plans and intentions do not always work out. We owned one center in north Houston that stayed remarkably well occupied despite a high crime rate. I made a deal with the Houston police department to fund a store front office, which they would occupy. The day the police moved in, several tenants moved out. Evidently, the tenants were making money selling illegal drugs and did not want to be located close to the police.

Our active redevelopment and repositioning programs required capital. Morgan Stanley provided additional working capital in the first year, but we secured bank lines led by Bank of America, Bank One, and Bank United to finance most of our development and redevelopment requirements. Later, Morgan Stanley helped us issue a commercial mortgage-backed security (CMBS) 10-year bond backed by our stabilized assets. I was also able to negotiate a deal with a U.S. pension fund, advised by AEW Capital Management, providing us equity for our new development venture.

The City of Houston cited CA for its contribution to the improvement of city neighborhoods. They even declared one day "Center America Day" in the city. The media frequently covered our neighborhood improvement projects.

Life in Houston was very different than San Diego. People were nice, but the weather was hot and humid and the outdoor lifestyle of southern California was replaced by an indoor air-conditioned life in Texas. Andrew and I moved to Houston first because Andrew was 14 years old and starting high school that fall, but he had band camp in August before school began. Nanuk, our dog, came with us. The first week in our new home, we lacked furniture but Andrew refused to stay in a hotel because he thought Nanuk would be lonely; we slept on the floor together – father, son, and dog.

We lived in a beautiful home in the small town of Bunker Hill, which was in the Memorial Drive area and relatively close to the city. It was not near my office and required a relatively long commute to work, but it was near good public schools, and Jill wanted to live in a "village" instead of the city. We had a terrific life in Houston, and I have many good memories of Andrew and Ross growing up and doing things together as a family.

Our house had a back set of stairs from the garage to a small apartment over the garage. The boys and their friends could hang out there without disturbing us in the main house. Sometimes I would go in the apartment in the morning to work out, using some exercise equipment I kept there, only to stumble over neighborhood boys who fell asleep the night before. It was such a contrast to my life at a similar age and made me feel really good about the quality of life my sons enjoyed.

Jill was elected to the City Council of Bunker Hill and was active in politics; Andrew played trumpet in the high school band, became interested in computers, and developed close friendships in high school. One year, I gave Andrew the parts to a computer, and he built the computer himself. Ross quickly developed a broad array of close friendships, played sports with friends, and enjoyed life. I co-coached Ross's baseball team and was home for dinner almost every night.

Nanuk made many friends in our cul-de-sac as he roamed the neighborhood, stopping at familiar neighbors and begging for treats. He learned how to let himself into George and Ann Quirk's home by head-butting their front door. He played with their dogs, and always found treats in their kitchen. Whenever I could not find Nanuk, I called the Quirks and asked that they send him home.

Other times, I would be looking for Nanuk, and Mexican workers overheard me and start shouting "Nanuk" in heavily accented Spanish. Usually, Nanuk would emerge from nearby after finishing a taco or burrito furnished by his Mexican friends.

Unfortunately, Nanuk died in Houston of old age, and an inability to walk or run due to hip dysplasia. It was one of my saddest days when Ross and I took Nanuk to the vet and stayed and held him while the doctor put him to sleep. I cried for hours afterward.

We never planned to stay long in Houston; it was a job that was supposed to last three years, but nothing ever works out just as planned. The turnaround of CA required seven years, and we lived in Houston until after Ross graduated from high school in 2004.

Eventually, we sold Center America to New Plan Excel Realty Trust (New Plan), a New York Stock Exchange (NYSE)-listed trust headed by my friend, Glenn Rufrano. The investors made a handsome return on their investment, MSREF achieved recognition and compensation for its successful investment, and the senior employees and I were well compensated for our contribution. The ingredients for success were very similar to those at PPA: focus, teamwork, alignment, capital structure, and commitment.

As part of the transaction, Glenn insisted I join New Plan as president and oversee the operational transformation of a highly centralized New York-centric company to a nationwide high-performance platform.

Recently I stopped by the old offices in Houston. It had been 10 years since Center America was a stand-alone company so this visit was a nostalgic journey for me. When I arrived, Linda McGee greeted me in the office, just like old times. Most of the employees remained with New Plan, and the Houston office became the headquarters for the southwest region of New Plan and then changed again to the regional office for Brixmor. Many of the employees are still working there today, making neighborhoods better, and providing investors with a good return.

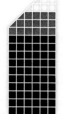

Chapter 21

NEW PLAN: CORPORATE RESTRUCTURE NEW YORK STYLE

My experience restructuring companies moved to a bigger arena in 2002. Working in New York City for a NYSE-listed company required reinventing an operating model in the public spotlight while maintaining quarterly earnings.

The cold winter wind swept across Bryant Park, sending a chill through both of us as we hurried to the restaurant on the park in midtown Manhattan. Inside, we took seats but were slow to remove our coats. Winter in New York can be bitter cold when the wind is blowing and channeling through the tall towers which populate New York City; it reminds me of Chicago.

I sat across the two-person table from Glenn Rufrano, a longtime friend and CEO of New Plan Excel Realty Trust. Glenn is a short man, then in his mid-50s, and balding. A native New Yorker of Italian parentage, he is also animated, smart, passionate, and full of energy.

I negotiated the deal to sell Center America to New Plan with Glenn two years earlier. As part of the deal, Glenn insisted that I join New Plan for at least three years. He was not prepared to buy 100 shopping centers without the guy who ran them; there was too much risk. So I joined New Plan in 2002 and signed a three-year employment contract.

"Scott, you and I both have a year left on our employment contracts. When we made the deal two years ago, I promised you I would step aside and you would be CEO with the board's support, which will not be a problem. I will become chairman and stay involved. But if you want to be CEO, you must move to New York; you cannot continue to commute from Houston every week. Do you want to be CEO?"

I worked in New York City from 2002 to 2005, commuting back to Houston every weekend. Jill did not want to move to New York or even visit me there. So I made the three- to four-hour flight every Monday morning, rising before dawn and arriving back every Friday evening for three years. It was a grueling schedule.

I thought about Glenn's generous offer. I knew being CEO of a well-known NYSE-listed REIT was a big deal and meant a lot of money. I guessed there was a potential paycheck of at least $25 million, especially if a particular deal we were discussing moved to reality.

"Glenn, it has been a good relationship, and we have accomplished much together. I think you really like being a public company CEO while I prefer to work outside the spotlight. I think you need to remain as CEO of New Plan."

I continued, "My wife will not move to New York. She has decided to move to San Diego, so if I want to stay married, I will have to leave New Plan next year and move with her." With that, I turned away from the biggest payday I could ever imagine. Some things are more important than money.

On a subsequent earnings call with analysts and investors, I announced I would be leaving New Plan at the end of my three-year contract. I said my wife had followed me throughout my career and it was now time for me to follow her and support her desire to move back to San Diego. I received many emails and calls afterward, and they divided into two groups. One group thought it was admirable to put personal commitments over career opportunity; the other and larger group thought I was nuts.

When I joined New Plan in 2002, its office was in midtown Manhattan, and the company did not have regional offices despite the national breadth of operations. It was centrally managed with all decisions made at the corporate office.

There is a picture, which is commonly sold in New York tourist shops and galleries as a print, which depicts the world centered on New York City with New Jersey somewhere in the distance. Nothing else exists. This, in a way, reflected the New Plan approach.

I felt strongly that we needed to decentralize key decision making and set up regional offices empowered with local staff. Staff based in Atlanta, for example, should be able to lease and manage centers in the Southeast more effectively than staff based in New York City. The local staff would better know the stores, the customers, and the brokers operating in the area. In my view, our national contacts would supplement local knowledge and local tenants to achieve best results.

As part of joining New Plan, Glenn and his staff agreed in advance to allow me to implement a regional operating platform, retaining centralized accounting, and financial reporting and monitoring. I would not have joined if this critical issue had not been resolved.

I set up offices in Atlanta, Georgia; Houston (the CA office); Philadelphia, Pennsylvania; Orlando, Florida; San Diego; and Detroit, Michigan. These cities reflected where our assets were located and the availability of good staff. I would have preferred Chicago to Detroit, for example, but Tom Litzler was a top-notch leader and would run the Midwest operations, but only if it were located in Detroit, near where he lived. Los Angeles would have been better than San Diego, geographically, but Rick Froese, an old colleague from the Hahn Company, was available in San Diego and would not move to Los Angeles. Having talented people whom you trust is key to a diffused operating corporate model.

Every year I visited each office multiple times and spent about a week reviewing every line of every budget, including leasing assumptions, rents, expenses, etc. When the boss is focused on details, the regional staff is even more focused and mistakes are rare.

One of the challenges of a company with great geographic diversity and regional management is learning and understanding the assets, the people, and the local issues. I visited every asset – there were eventually about 500 centers – many located in small towns across the United States. I relied heavily on Hertz navigation systems to find my way, which occasionally led to unanticipated results.

One night, my colleague Mike Carroll and I were driving through South Carolina in heavy rain, and I was having difficulty following the road with such limited visibility. The navigation system directed us to a parking garage far from where we were going. We reset the system and searched for our shopping center, but the navigation system kept redirecting us to the car park. Mike, who subsequently became CEO of the successor company, Brixmor, and I believed the car wanted to get out of the heavy rain and sought refuge in the car park. We still laugh about this incident years later when we get together.

Another time, Mike and I met with Wal-Mart executives in Bentonville, Arkansas, and the meeting went late into the afternoon. We had promised our managers of properties in the nearby Ozark mountains, that we would visit them that evening. I did not want to disappoint our on-site managers, who were almost never visited by New York-based executives.

We drove to Branson, Missouri, and had a late dinner with the manager of our property there. Then we began driving north to the Lakes of the Ozarks district, where we had another mall. Mike called the manager and told her we may not be there until 2 a.m., but she met us with a pot of coffee, and we toured the property with her staff in the early hours of the morning. For many months afterword, the employee grapevine was filled with stories about Mike and me inspecting properties at 2 a.m. and 3 a.m., showing interest and dedication by all involved.

Months later I was visiting Roanoke, Virginia, and had a late dinner with Mike DeGidio, our property manager there. When I asked if he would show me his property portfolio beginning at about 11 p.m., he said he had already told his wife I was in town and he would not be home until the morning. I had a reputation of having a keen interest in what our staff was doing, our properties, and how I could support their efforts. It almost became a badge of honor to be out late with me talking about property issues and opportunities in towns throughout the country.

There are always issues with running a regional model, and oftentimes it has to do with people. One time we received a formal complaint of sexual harassment in one of the regions. An assistant complained that the head of the office was having an affair and favoring his mistress at work. This was a serious charge, and our HR director and corporate counsel responded with a visit and series of interviews. They returned to New York in total confusion. Nothing made sense. The testimony of various people in the office was contradictory in multiple ways. We were unsure what to do.

I flew there and met first with the head of the office at a nearby restaurant.

"Joe [not real name], I hired you, I promoted you, and I gave you a chance. You have done really well. Now I need to know what the hell is going on around here. If you are completely honest with me, I will help you no matter what the outcome. If I think you are lying to me, you will not have a job when I walk out of here, and you will have trouble finding a job in the future. Talk to me. Straight."

Joe told an amazing story. Yes, he was having an affair but the allegation was wrong. The accuser had all her facts wrong and had made up most of her story. Various employees testified that she was not truthful; other employees testified falsely to help Joe because they felt sorry for him and thought the accuser was not credible. Various employees said they saw Joe at various times at various places. Obviously there was no conspiracy because no one's story matched.

I met with all the affected employees individually and put them all on notice. Any more lies or misbehavior, and they would be fired without appeal. The accuser resigned a month later claiming mental distress, and we agreed and paid her for her distress. Joe went back to his wife and is still married many years later and has a great family. There was never a problem with that office again. Everyone accepted that they had a second chance and watched out for each other to make sure none of the teammates ever strayed again.

Sometimes a second chance is warranted. Other times, violation is clear and the employee must be terminated. At Hahn, I fired the regional head of Hahn Southwestern operations when he took advantage of his secretary, having an affair and then trying to cover it up.

The regional operating platform proved a big success at New Plan. The company expanded to over 500 shopping centers across multiple states. We were positioned for growth and out-performance.

A couple of years after I left the company, Centro Properties bought New Plan. Glenn received more than $50 million, according to published reports. Centro announced that it was paying for the assets and the regional operating platform, which it valued at more than $300 million. I received a call when I was in San Diego shortly after the acquisition had been announced. It was Arnold Lubach, former CEO of New Plan before Glenn.

"Scott, it's Arnold. I just called to say 'thank you.' I am a rich man and my family will be well taken care of thanks to the reorganization you put in place." Arnold was being a bit generous; Glenn and the team drove the business to success, but the recognition felt good.

Ironically, Centro's acquisition of New Plan and its failure to fund the acquisition resulted in the bankruptcy of Centro. Glenn Rufrano became CEO of Centro and lived in Australia during the reorganization. We often came together and shared stories about New York and life in Australia.

Chapter 22

CLARENDON HOMES: BUILDING NICE HOMES WHILE LOSING MONEY

As we struggled with Investa's financing woes, we were also confronted with a plethora of operating issues. The most significant of these was our homebuilding subsidiary, Clarendon.

There is an old story about the two American hillbillies from rural Indiana, Jeb and Sam. They decide to go into business selling watermelons. The plan was to buy directly from farmers in Indiana, drive to the big city (Chicago), and sell them, cutting out the middleman and retaining the profit. They drove their truck to local farms and bought watermelons for an average of $1 each. They then drove to Chicago and tried to sell their melons for $2 each, but were surprised to find the big grocery stores were only charging 85 cents. So they dropped their price to 75 cents each and sold the whole load in a couple hours.

Jeb turned to Sam, "What do you think, Sam? We sold the whole load in two hours. Pretty good, huh?"

But Sam asked, "Jeb, we paid $1 each and sold them for 75 cents. How are we going to make money?"

"Volume, Sam. We are going to make it up in volume!"

Clarendon was a top-quality homebuilder, headquartered in New South Wales, and owned by Investa. The division had a leading market share (i.e., volume) and a sterling reputation. It also lost money consistently.

When I arrived at Investa, there were six separate operating divisions including Office, Funds Management, Clarendon Homes, Development, Corporate, and Project Enterprise. About half the employees were at Clarendon, which was a custom homebuilder headquartered in a suburban Norwest business center near Sydney.

As Investa's senior management discussed issues and activities, it appeared to me that most of our discussion always drifted back to Clarendon. This homebuilder and land development company made no money despite its quality reputation, and we seemed to be consumed with a never-ending list of problems.

In my business experience, I have found it is often the case that the problem division, which makes no money, dominates management time and attention. When we should be focused on how to maximize our advantage in profitable areas, we are bogged down in problem-solving, money-losing issues.

I have always disliked home building as a business endeavor. It is a business typically with very low profit margins and almost no barriers to entry, leading to high levels of competition. In the good times, builders make some money; in the bad times, they can lose lots of money.

I worked for a homebuilder in Philadelphia in 1976 and quit after one year. Big corporations cannot compete with small family builders who operate with minimal overhead and low profit margins. In my view, big homebuilders survive utilizing clever accounting practices. But Investa's focus was on cash flow; favorable accounting did nothing for us.

Someone once explained the business to me: "A family builder will gather everyone around the table at year end. The father, say his name is 'Ralph' will say something like, 'Boys we had a great year. We built $250 million of houses and we made $2 million for ourselves. Let's celebrate and hope the next year will be as good.'"

So Ralph is thrilled with less than a 1 percent profit margin while a big corporate builder needs a 15 percent margin. If a corporate builder actually achieved desired margins, Ralph's cousins and friends would all start into the business and offer homes for less cost (and lower profit), driving down profits. Anyone with a pickup truck and a tool bag can go into the home-building business.

In good times, volumes increase, giving bigger builders an opportunity to realize efficiencies of scale. However, the real estate industry is a cycle, and good times are always followed by bad times. The scale efficiencies work in reverse when volumes fall. The production structure for producing 1,000 homes a year cannot be slightly adjusted when volumes fall to 500 homes. A completely new model is necessary.

I met with Clarendon senior staff early in my tenure at Investa. They seemed disorganized and unwilling to consider changes to the business model reflecting lower volumes. There was no CEO for the division and the former Investa CEO apparently never visited the Clarendon offices. The Clarendon guys were drifting and losing money.

At one point, I visited some of the display units Clarendon offered prospective retail customers and engaged with the sales agents. I was surprised to learn none of the displays could be sold because they did not meet local government building codes. We had display units to show customers, but then had to tell them that they were not allowed to buy if they liked what they saw. This was bizarre but reflected the lack of investment in the business. Older display homes had not been replaced.

Things appeared desperate. Clarendon was hemorrhaging cash that Investa needed for paying our bills. I had to act quickly. In my deal with Sonny and the MSREF guys, I did not have cash to cover operating deficits in the housing business.

I appointed Maurice Felizzi, the then-CFO, as CEO of Clarendon. Maurice was a good numbers guy and understood the importance of managing the cash flow better. However, he was not a detailed housing guy steeped in the tradition of cost cutting and negotiations with suppliers.

Maurice called a meeting of his senior staff, and I joined them early one Monday morning. I thanked them for their continued effort but gave them the following direction: "Investa cannot continue to support Clarendon if it continues to lose money. We do not have the time to wait for volumes to return. You must learn to make money at current volumes, even if it means changing how you do business. Everyone in this room knows more about the housing business here than I do, so I don't have the solution. The answer must come from you. I am leaving on a business trip out of town and will not return until Friday. If you cannot come up with a reasonable plan to make money, I am closing the business when I return. You have until Friday. I am hopeful you will find a way."

Then I left.

Actually, I could not just close the business, but I needed to send the Clarendon team a strong message. Morgan Stanley's Sydney office continued to believe the residential market would recover soon, home-building volumes would rebound, and Clarendon's entity value would be restored. They objected to any discussion of closure. We also had the problem of home warranty legislation, which left Clarendon or its successor liable for future claims from homebuyers.

Maurice and his team, with help from Michelle Dance of Investa and James Quigley of Morgan Stanley, worked for three days examining the production process, staffing, costs, margins, and likely volumes. They redefined the model and formulated a plan that included a 25 percent reduction in staff. I reviewed the plan the following Monday and gave it a "green light."

I also instructed Jonathan Callaghan to separate Clarendon legally from Investa with the view that we could spin it off and refocus Investa's efforts on our office and land portfolios. Finally, I pulled the land development group from Clarendon and brought them over to Investa, merging them with the land development group at Investa, providing efficiencies and synergies with the two staffs. Clarendon became a simple, clean homebuilder, and Investa became a simplified company with three business lines at the time: office, funds management, and land development.

In December of 2008, we spun Clarendon off, and it became a stand-alone company. It had its own board, an experienced, independent chairman (Michael Cochran), and fully serviced staff. I thought this was the end of the story as far as Investa was concerned. I was wrong.

Because Clarendon had no history of making money, the banks were unwilling to provide financing. As a result, Clarendon continued to rely on Investa to finance its operations.

In 2009, Clarendon's pursuit of profits remained elusive. It lost more money. Volumes continued to fall along with margins. The company no longer had a land inventory to mask part of its losses because the land had been transferred to Investa's land development group.

We were approached by a Japanese homebuilder who wanted to buy a home-building operation in Australia. Maurice and I negotiated with them and discussions progressed. I thought they may be willing to pay $100 million for Clarendon, which would have been a good outcome, but we were unable to finalize the deal, and the Japanese company bought AVJennings' homebuilding operations for, reportedly, about $35 million.

Clarendon continued to lose money in 2010. Maurice was unable to stop the bleeding. He started a Projects division to build housing for other developers with the hope of making profits to offset losses in the custom-building business. Then in 2011 the sky fell in.

The Projects division had taken on many new projects and bid aggressively to win the work. The projects were almost all delivered over budget, resulting in high losses – about $30 million. We did not have the money to cover these unexpected losses. Investa sold our Retail Funds division, for which I did not see much of a future, for about $40 million, and those proceeds effectively paid for Clarendon's growing losses. It put considerable pressure on our balance sheet and cash flow at the same time we were struggling to refinance the office portfolio loans.

In addition to an adverse market and higher-than-supportable operating costs, Clarendon obviously did not have good financial controls. This made the future outlook even more clouded.

We continued to try to sell the business without success. Maurice retrenched more employees and reduced costs, but he was just following the losses instead of getting out in front and reconfiguring the company for even lower-volume levels. Clarendon threatened to destabilize Investa's survival plan.

In late 2012, we worked out a deal to give Clarendon to another homebuilder; we literally paid someone to take Clarendon. Ultimately, Clarendon was worthless despite maintaining a good reputation and building quality homes. And along the way, it drained a significant amount of desperately needed cash and diverted time and attention from more productive endeavors.

Not everything in business works as it should despite careful planning. We thought with focus and attention, our homebuilding business could restructure and achieve profitability. In hindsight, the operation was unable to adjust its cost structure quickly enough to meet market declines in home buying, and we should have exited the business much sooner.

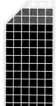

Chapter 23

INTERNATIONAL GLOBE-TROTTING BUT TROUBLES AT HOME

Jill and I began to spend more time in Del Mar, California, near San Diego in 2005 after I finished my work at New Plan. First, we lived in a condominium we had owned as a second home for years, and then we bought a house near the village in downtown Del Mar.

I began an exciting career as a consultant. Wherever an investor client had problem projects or companies that were underperforming, they asked me to visit and recommend a fix. I worked on projects in China, India, Turkey, the Netherlands, the United Kingdom, Poland, Germany, Portugal, Mexico, and Canada. In 2006, I lived in London for six months and worked primarily with a Netherlands-based company with operations throughout Europe and Turkey. I found a flat in the trendy neighborhood of South Kensington. It was far from Canary Wharf, where my office was, but I wanted Jill to be happy and enjoy the nearby shops and museums. She joined me for a few months in London before returning to Del Mar to be closer to her friends. It was a fascinating professional time for me with exposure to a variety of properties and cultures, and the challenge of improving their performance.

In my travels, I was surprised by the consistent themes that ran throughout property development and operations across countries and cultures, but there were also distinct differences. A few of the many vignette postcards from abroad follow.

China. I spent a couple of weeks with clients looking at retail development opportunities in China. The opportunity afforded by the urbanization of the population and extraordinary levels of growth was incredible, but the risks were also substantial.

Virtually all dinners we had with Chinese partners, investors, and colleagues were 10-course banquets. Most of the courses consisted of food of unknown origin or recognizable form. After a couple of courses, I stopped asking what the food was that I was supposed to eat because I did not want to be viewed as culturally insensitive.

At one large banquet, each place setting had Western knives and forks as well as chopsticks. I observed that all the Chinese participants were using Western silverware and all the Westerners were using chopsticks. Everyone was striving to be sensitive to each other's cultural differences.

All formal meals included shots of potent alcohol and many toasts. Once I asked the president of Wal-Mart in China what was his biggest challenge. I thought he would say distribution network or import issues, but he said "drinking." Russia is similar with its vodka consumption but in a less formal way.

In Shanghai, we sat in a series of meetings dealing with a proposed new retail development project. The Chinese developer partner, a short, animated man with passable English, was presenting a novel plan. We were unimpressed, but were sensitive to being overly critical or confrontational. At one point, I asked if the proposed tenant space posed any leasing challenges since it lacked good access or visibility. Had we been in the U.S., I would have been far less diplomatic. "No," the developer replied. "It should lease well."

Later that night, we visited a project done by the same developer that was similar in nature. Unfortunately, it was largely vacant. Access and tenant space layouts were terrible. When we questioned the local partner who did the deal and was very optimistic, all we received was pushback and complaints that as Westerners we knew nothing about China. Oftentimes, when someone disagrees, they use the appearance of cultural insensitivity to mask project deficiencies; this is not just true in China but seems common elsewhere.

The project was ultimately developed unsuccessfully, and a local partner was later convicted of bribing local government officials and hiding his personal ownership in the same project we questioned. Corruption is endemic in many parts of the world, and I was so naïve.

I am still awed by the growth in China. Every year, the Beijing area increases population by about 250,000 people, and Shanghai increases by about 400,000 residents a year. Traffic congestion was bad in Beijing, so they built new highways right through older, well-developed areas and had commenced construction of six subway lines concurrently. Developed countries in the West would have had to undertake years of studies and decades of plans to build a single urban highway or subway line. In China, everything moves at high speed.

When I asked how they could build a highway through such a highly developed area so quickly, I was told that it was not a problem. First, the government puts the highway on the five-year plan. It is not open to discussion or debate. Then they send notices to the affected residents and business owners, telling them when to vacate and how much they will be paid for their property and relocation. There is no venue for protest or complaint.

I was also surprised at the level of control the government exerted on the flow of information. We generally did not talk about politics with our Chinese colleagues, but one evening, after drinks and dinner, I asked a Chinese colleague what she thought of the U.S. She was a brilliant woman, well educated with an MBA, very literate and articulate in English. Her response shocked me.

"We respect the U.S. but we do not like their tendency to intervene militarily in foreign affairs."

I asked, "I understand Vietnam, but where else has the U.S. intervened militarily?"

She said, "Korea."

"But, Korea intervention was led by the United Nations and was in response to the invasion of the South by the North."

"No," she replied. "North Korea was merely resettling some people when the U.S. and their allies attacked."

She really believed this because this is what she was taught in school and had no access to contradictory and more accurate information.

We should never assume the Chinese people have access to correct history or public affairs; what they receive is politically motivated and access to contrary information is tightly controlled.

I never thought economic freedom could be decoupled from political freedom. I thought free enterprise was the twin of political democracy. China seems to have proved this assumption incorrect, at least for now.

India. I made multiple trips to India looking at various development proposals and meeting with partners and potential partners. I formed several impressions.

First, the government has held back economic progress for decades through socialist policies, corruption, and bureaucracy. The Indians I met were hard workers, valued education, and were entrepreneurial. I believe if the government had not been so obstructionist, India's living standards would be on a level with developed Western countries.

The Indian businessmen I met were generally determined to do things their way and preferred not to take advice from Westerners or learn from the mistakes we have made over time. They will make their own mistakes and learn accordingly; unfortunately, this is unnecessary.

I met with the head of an Indian department store. He asked what I thought of the recent boom in shopping center developments in India. I replied, "I suspect two-thirds of the shopping centers being developed in India will fail. They are not well conceived or planned."

He replied, "I think the percentage may be more like 90 percent."

I met with one developer in Pune. His project was under construction and about half-built. After looking through his plans, I asked, "Where is the parking?"

"It is on one level underground," he replied.

"But, there are not many spaces, and this is a big mall," I asked.

"Parking is expensive. Maybe people will take the bus."

The buses in Pune were very old and dilapidated; they exclusively served the poor. The mall was a fashion statement targeted at the newly wealthy and the aspirational shoppers. These target customers were not going to take the bus.

Another time I met with the developer and his team to discuss a proposed shopping mall in Amritsar. I told them they needed more access points to the big shopping mall; there was only one access street for all the cars, and it would almost certainly become clogged and inhibit shoppers from visiting the mall.

The site planner argued against providing additional entrances. Finally, the reason emerged. He declared, "If we have more than one access point, it will be harder for security to identify and intercept Pakistani terrorists from reaching the mall." It is important to understand cultural and geopolitical contexts when working in foreign countries, and India is no exception. Amritsar is located in the state of Punjab, which lies next to the border with Pakistan, and sensitivities are very high concerning security.

The infrastructure in India is generally awful. The major highways are typically two lanes each way, and cars compete for driving space with trucks, motorbikes, auto rickshaws, bicycles, tractors, horses, donkeys, elephants, and camels. Driving through one town, the highway narrowed to one lane each way as newly constructed shacks encroached on the pavement. There was a big demonstration going on, and I asked what was happening.

My driver told me some government officials wanted to force the squatters to move back off the road, and they and their relatives and friends were holding a political protest rally, with local politicians in attendance. Everyone votes in India, including the homeless, so the poor can easily block infrastructure projects and often do so.

Another time in New Delhi, I needed to replace my lost reading glasses and asked where I could by a new pair. "Not today," replied my host. "All stores in Delhi are on strike."

"Why?" I asked.

"Because the government has asked the stores to post their occupancy permits and most do not have one. So every store closes until the government rescinds their decree. Don't worry, the government will rescind it tomorrow." The government did back off the next day and the stores reopened.

In Mumbai, the poor people build shacks along major streets taking right-of-way that had been reserved for future expansion of the arterials. When enough shacks were constructed, the city would build public toilets for the new community. Typically, shacks are two levels with a ladder accessing the second floor apartment, and the government clearly accepted this type of housing as a permanent addition.

The sanitation conditions in India are not first-world quality, and everyone I know (including me) who goes there becomes sick at some point. On my first trip, I sat in an airport lounge waiting for a connecting flight to Mumbai from Delhi. An Indian man across from me introduced himself. He lived in Houston, Texas, but his family was still in India.

"How often do you come for a visit?" I asked.

"About every four years. I would like to visit more, but I always get very sick when I visit," he replied.

Another time I was sitting in the airport in Bangalore, and there were mosquitoes buzzing around me. I was conflicted; I did not want to risk being bitten and possibly contracting dengue fever, which was reportedly widespread, but I did not want to go on a killing rampage without knowing if reincarnation could mean these insects were the spirits of people, and it would be bad form for a foreigner to annihilate them. The mosquitoes did not seem to be disturbing the Indian passengers, so I moved to another part of the airport where there seemed to be fewer pests.

A few months later, I saw John Waters, an old friend in San Diego. He told me he and his family had recently returned from a trip to India. It was a great trip, but his daughter contracted dengue fever; she was fortunate to be back in the U.S. before she became ill.

I asked if they knew where she had been bitten, and John told me they were quite certain it was at the airport in Bangalore.

India should not be considered in the same context as China. One is chaotic, lacks infrastructure, has no viable plans for growth or development, and is a democracy. The other has first-world infrastructure, has an economy that employs millions of new workers annually, lays out specific development plans and implements them every five years, and has a Communist government. It is questionable which government has better served its people.

Turkey. I enjoyed my many trips to Turkey very much. Istanbul is one of the great cities of the world, spanning and connecting Europe to Asia. The Turkish coastline is beautiful, and Ephesus is an amazing restored part of world history. Culturally, there are some differences, however.

At a conference in France, a Turkish competitor in the shopping center business came up to me and complained that a company owned by my clients in Turkey was operating dishonestly and unethically.

"Are they paying bribes to officials?" I asked, fearing the answer.

He replied, "Bribes are not unethical; everyone pays bribes."

"What are they doing, then?" I asked curiously.

"They are using leverage by offering tenants space in good projects to take space in challenged projects, and this is unfair to others who do not have good projects."

So what is unethical in business clearly differs by culture.

One time, I was travelling through the interior of Turkey. We took a flight to Denizli. Only a few flights a day travel to Denizli from Istanbul because it has a military airport that is closed part of each day for military flights. Denizli seemed to be in the middle of nowhere. From the airport, the land is barren with salt flats providing some relief. It lies almost 200 kilometers from Izmir, which represents the nearest port.

Yet Denizli is filled with factories, many owned by well-known Western companies, manufacturing a variety of goods for shipment to Western consumers. There was one factory that was relocating from the U.S.; I read about it in the American newspapers. It amazed me that it was evidently more cost efficient to make things in the middle of Turkey, send the products to Izmir by truck, send them to a U.S. port by ship, and then ship them from the port to the U.S. destination than it was to make the products in the U.S. I know proximity to consumers in Europe was also a factor, but I was still shocked.

I suspect Turkey has suffered significantly from Europe's more recent economic decline and the disruptions in the nearby Middle East, but I will always be impressed by the work ethic and dynamic business environment in Turkey. Unfortunately for my client, the charismatic Turkish CEO was terminated when it was discovered he was padding the payroll with relatives and reportedly taking kickbacks from vendors. This is a common problem throughout developing countries and underscores the difficult trade-offs between bringing in ex-patriots from the home country to manage everything according to home country standards or hiring more local staff, who are more knowledgeable in local practices and customs. There is a balance, but it is often hard to find the best balance point.

Europe. I worked with Multi-Development Company (Multi), which was based in Gouda in the Netherlands, for six months when I was located in London in 2006. Multi was run by its founder and chairman, Hans van Veggel, who was a dynamic and successful Dutch businessman. Hans' passion was architecture and creating beautiful shopping malls.

Unfortunately, the company suffered from poor financial controls and oversight. As long as the European economies were in good shape and Multi made money by developing and selling new malls, no one in the company seemed to care that normal risk management standards were not maintained. My client, who purchased an interest in the company in 2006, was concerned, however, and asked me to spend time with management and their asset management staff.

It was a futile effort in my judgment, because Hans had been a very successful entrepreneur and did not fear failure that could arise from an economic downturn. Entrepreneurs are typically risk takers who embrace success and discount the possibility of failure. They make money when markets are favorable and struggle when markets turn negative.

My first meeting with the Multi executive team was as part of an investment committee meeting to approve the development of a new office building in Amsterdam. The rest of my client's team had not arrived due to a late plane, so I was alone among the Dutch company members.

The chairman asked if I had any questions before they approved the deal. I asked what the creditworthiness of the primary tenant was; I knew it was a risky credit because I had checked, but I wondered if anyone at Multi had bothered to inquire. No one on the investment committee appeared to know the answer but didn't think it was relevant since the proposed building was well located, pre-leased, and architecturally handsome. When I pursued the line of inquiry, the chairman walked out of the meeting.

Over time, it became clear the Dutch were not about to take advice from Americans or British investor representatives. I learned the way to improve operations was to meet and talk frequently with Dutch executives and plant seeds of change through questions or stories of other firms and the things they did to improve. If the Dutch guys thought it was their idea, it had a chance. Eventually, financial controls and models were introduced and cash flow forecasting improved, but it was a slow process. When the GFC hit in full vengeance two years later, Multi defaulted on its debt.

My investor client asked me to consider becoming CEO of Multi before I returned to the U.S. from London. Jill would never agree to live in Europe and so I declined. Subsequently, I was asked to call a very talented former colleague in London, and encourage him to take the CEO job. He had been offered a good deal but was asking for more compensation – comparable to what he would have earned at his present job. My client thought I may be able to talk him into accepting, which they had been unable to do.

I sent my friend and former colleague a one-line email quoting a favorite saying of mine:

"Pigs get fed and hogs get eaten."

The next day, he accepted the job offer. When my client called to ask how I convinced the new CEO to accept the job offer, I declined to elaborate.

Mexico. I worked on several projects in Mexico throughout the years. At Hahn, I worked with Mexican partners to develop plans for a mall in Mexico City. When I was with Center America in Houston, we worked with a local Mexican partner and H-E-B grocery stores to develop neighborhood shopping centers in Mexico. I also was involved with a variety of proposals for various investors. Doing business in Mexico is different, but the Mexican people are gracious, fun, and welcoming. They take time to get to know you before you can even discuss doing a deal. Time moves more slowly, perhaps because of all the tequila and big meals. I liked going there very much, even when the crime rate escalated with the growing power of drug lords.

When walking across a construction site with the senior executive of Saks Fifth Avenue department store, we were careful not to fall into the holes in the concrete or trip over the many impediments. I asked the general counsel of the Mexican development company whose fault it would be if the Saks guy fell to his death. He replied, "Legally, it would be his fault. He is the one who fell into the hole; no one pushed him."

Another time I was with Ernie Hahn (founder and chairman of the Hahn Company), Bill Dillard Jr. (CEO of Dillard Department Stores), and John Gilchrist (CEO of the Hahn Company). We were in a van travelling on the ring highway, or Periférico, in Mexico City when our van broke down on the inside lane.

"What do we do now?" I asked the driver.

"Run for it," he responded.

So Ernie, Bill, John, and I ran across multiple lanes of traffic avoiding fast cars to reach safety. I felt like an illegal immigrant. Evidently, Mexican drivers are accustomed to avoiding pedestrians running across highways.

One time I met with our Mexican lawyers. I had talked with a shopping center competitor about their efforts to develop a mall that would be competitive to one we were thinking of developing. I was concerned we could be violating anti-competitive laws. He assured me Mexico had no such laws.

Another time I was walking with a friend and owner of a shopping center company in Mexico. The most important thing, he told me, was to obtain a favorable tax valuation when you develop a new property. After the first valuation, the value will increase automatically every year by the official inflation rate, so the starting value is key to future financial success.

"How do we obtain a favorable valuation?" I asked.

"I go to the senior tax assessor's home on a weekend, and we drink some tequila. I notice he likes to watch football but his television is small. So I buy him a big television and send it to him as a gift."

"We cannot do business that way. Bribing officials is illegal. Is there another way?" I asked.

"Not that is effective," was the response.

I worked on another possible deal with a Mexican executive I had also become friendly with. I called my friend and told him, "If you want to do this deal, you will have to show the U.S. investors your financial books."

He replied, "Which books?"

"How many sets of books do you have?" I asked.

"Three sets. Everyone in Mexico has three sets of books. One is for the government, one is for investors, and one is for the family. No one sees the family books except the family members."

Unfortunately, for all the time I spent in Mexico, I never did a deal there. A client did one deal that I know of, and I helped with some of the negotiations.

Russia. I have made many trips to Russia and have had many experiences. Moscow appears to be a dynamic urban city but with an undercurrent of crime and seediness. One night I was walking down a main boulevard with a few Russian colleagues and passed a dozen young women lined up in two parallel lines. "Ivan, what is this?" I asked my Russian colleague.

"They are prostitutes waiting for an oligarch, who will choose which ones he wants," was the reply.

Another time I was with some colleagues from New York and some Russian partners. We went to a Western-style pub in Moscow. It could have been in any American or Australian city except for the fact that most of the patrons were women. Soon after we entered, we were deluged by women making inquiries, trying their limited English skills, or suggesting we buy them a drink. "Igor, are these prostitutes?" I inquired.

"No," he replied. "They are just single women who want to meet foreigners and find a way to a better life."

My trip to the cities of Siberia in 2008 just before I started at Investa was a fascinating experience. The vast geographic scope of Siberia is hard to comprehend. It encompasses seven time zones. I was traveling with executives from a Russian property development company, French investors, a German-born colleague who spoke English, and a translator who knew English, Russian, and French. We had a private jet to access the far-flung cities, each connected to the other by the Trans-Siberian Railway.

At the end of every day, regardless of the city, we would gather in some Russian restaurant, typically around a big wooden table, with the local staff of the development company. The dinners were hearty food with meats and starches, piled in bowls and on plates. Vodka glasses were filled and refilled as soon as they were emptied.

The Russian hosts started the toasts, which went throughout the meal and late into the night. The French and English toasts were usually short, but the Russian toasts often became long stories. By late in the night, the Russian speakers often forgot how they started the toast but meandered along anyway. We all bonded and laughed a lot, but the drinking was difficult on the bodies. I suspect this way of doing business results in shorter life spans.

In restaurants where we were asked to order a main course, I usually asked for a local recommendation. At one dinner, the Russian CEO of RosEvro, Ivan Sitnikov, insisted I try the local fish, which I did. The fish were very tasty, but I could not place the spices or flavors so I asked where the fish were from.

Ivan laughed and said, "Scott, do you remember the dirty river that runs through town? The pollution gives the fish a special flavor."

I gathered that eating polluted fish with a sprinkling of heavy metals and PCB chemicals provided the unusual flavor combination. Fortunately, we moved on the next day and I avoided eating fish the remainder of the trip. But the Russians did not seem bothered; maybe the high levels of vodka killed the bad stuff in the food.

While in Siberia, we stopped in the city of Novosibirsk, with a population of about one million. About 30 kilometers outside of Novosibirsk, tucked into the dense forest, was another city encompassing a university, several science research labs, and perhaps 90,000 people. Evidently, Stalin set up this remote and isolated center of science and research to work on projects like the nuclear bomb, where workers would be totally focused on their work and isolated from Westerners. This virtually hidden scientific outpost continues today, although it has become better known and has even successfully sought Western capital to fund certain research projects.

More recently, I worked on an investment in two big Russian shopping malls, including one in Saint Petersburg. Saint Petersburg is one of the most beautiful cities of the world and very European and old world in character. The many restored churches and museums are amazing places to visit and absorb the ornate qualities and craftsmanship as well as the breadth of the art.

I was surprised at how much shopper traffic the shopping malls attracted; colleagues explained that when the U.S.S.R. dissolved, everyone was given his or her apartment at no cost, so very few residents have mortgage or housing costs. Many do not own cars because of the lack of parking in the cities. With no housing or car expenses, and free or inexpensive schools, residents typically have considerable spending money for patronizing the malls and restaurants.

I was also surprised that mall tenants reported relatively low sales but continued to occupy high rent spaces and even renewed their leases when they came due. Finally, I figured out the tenants were understating their sales and success. We stopped using rent-to-sales as a measure of tenant health, which is how it is used in the Western world of shopping centers.

Home. Back in Del Mar, things were not going well. Jill became very dissatisfied with our relationship and turned her anger toward me, resulting in constant criticisms, put-downs, an insistence on separate bedrooms and eventually, separation. I found myself hiding from her to avoid confrontation. I had left the everyday work environment, where I had enjoyed considerable respect and acknowledgment for my skill and knowledge. The contrast between the friendly and supportive environs of work and the negative messages at home certainly contributed to my unhappiness and desire to withdraw.

One of my core values is the fundamental belief that life must be balanced between commitments to work and family responsibilities. I have spent decades of my life committed to achieving success in business while being there for my family. As the hostility escalated at home, I sought to withdraw as I did when my mother was so critical during my teen years. Clearly, my retreat did not help solve the issues between us.

I naïvely believed taking on an assignment in Australia would improve our relationship by eliminating the daily confrontations. Distance would allow her to realize I was not the source of her problems and discontent, my self-serving reasoning concluded. I was wrong; Jill filed for divorce just before Christmas of 2008, and the divorce was finalized in 2009. In my soul searching which followed, I struggled to understand how I missed the mark so badly and failed to understand the deeper aspects of marriage and relationships.

It is particularly ironic because I am very committed to ensuring professional women have equal access and opportunities in business. Listening to my mother talk about discrimination against women in the bank where she worked made me very sensitive to the need for fair and equal treatment.

I have been proactive in appointing women to senior executive positions throughout my career. More recently, I appointed Ming Long as CFO and then lobbied for her appointment to fund manager of IOF. I appointed one of the first chairwoman to a listed fund in Australia when I appointed Debbie Page to chair IOF.

My observations that follow about women are unrelated to the workplace but affect the relationships between partners and how differences result. After my divorce, I sought out others who had divorced after long-term marriages. I was surprised at the common themes and circumstances, which characterized virtually all of these divorces. Based on these discussions with older divorced men and women, I have drawn some observations, which some would characterize as overgeneralizations, but they may be helpful to others.

I realized, belatedly, that men and women are so different. We think differently; we arrive at decisions and conclusions taking different paths. In addition, our values and priorities are often not closely aligned, and our interpretations of events in which we are both participants can and do vary widely.

A fundamental mistake we make is assuming our partner is like us and not recognizing the differences which divide us. As young people, we cannot know this; as we age, recognition is often too late as our paths have diverged.

The women I met typically remembered past arguments, perceived slights or criticisms, harsh words said in anger, and disappointments, and they retained these bad memories, sometimes letting them accumulate and build up over time. Women keep score. After 30 years, Jill certainly was able to recall incidents in which she felt unappreciated or slighted.

By contrast, the men I talked with seemed to move on after disputes and not retain those angry memories. Typically, men do not keep score. For men, what happened yesterday is more important; for women, what happened yesterday must be seen in the context of what happened 10 years ago. It is not surprising we often do not recognize the issues that confront us, and we interpret events so differently.

It appears to me that men and women age differently as well. Men seem to be more easily content with the routine of the status quo; the certain knowledge and familiarity of shared experiences and memories, and the mutual interdependence that comes from a long partnership.

As women age, their bodies and hormones seem to change more radically than those of men. They reflect on what caused discontent in earlier years, on past unhappiness, and on the deficiencies of their partners. If they were stay-at-home moms, they may resent the loss of careers and the professions they gave up while their spouses were able to pursue theirs.

Women seem less content to continue an unsatisfactory relationship. They want something more from life. Too often, they turn their frustrations into anger directed at their partner.

These divergent attitudes and circumstances lead to late-in-life conflict. When the children are gone, there is no buffer or need for mutual focus and cooperation. The differences that were always there, but were suppressed for the sake of the children or the need to achieve financial independence, come back with nothing to divert their force.

I thought creating financial well-being for my family and being very involved with parental responsibilities were the keys to a successful family life. Jill clearly expected much more, and became critical and hostile when I did not live up to her expectations.

In the busy lives we lead and the demands that we all confront each day, emotional connections and communication are difficult challenges. We are different; we have little free time; we are tired. Life marches on with or without understanding, life as we know it stops, and we realize how far apart our journeys have taken us. We thought we were still next to each other. We realized how little we talked on our journey about deeper, interpersonal issues and feelings, and how little we knew about what happened inside each other. By then, it was too late.

Chapter 24

SUCCESSION

Investa was evolving and changing by late 2012. The death-defying corporate gymnastics, which allowed us to survive the GFC, would give way to a more "normal" business operation. Our continual crisis management ethos needed to change to a sustainable and efficient operating platform. At the same time, I was tired and anticipating a slower pace of life, at least semi-retirement. But I needed to prepare and position the company for the future before I could step back.

In November 2012, Hoke Slaughter and I met in the Axis Bar at the Mandarin Oriental Hotel in Marina Square in Singapore. It was winter in the Northern Hemisphere, but Singapore is always warm and humid, and this day was no different. The bar overlooked the dynamic Singapore skyline filled with tall buildings and cranes birthing even more skyscrapers on reclaimed coastline. I arrived early, as is typical, and Hoke ran a few minutes late, also as is typical. We have known each other for about 25 years, and conversation between us is easy and familiar, even when dealing with difficult challenges.

After a few pleasantries, Hoke asked the question I was expecting, "So, Scott, how long are you staying at Investa?"

"Hoke," I began. "We need to complete the refinancing of the Hold Portfolio this month and then we need to refinance the land loan or MOF again before next June. After that, the Investa platform is stable and de-risked. We have great people, and it is about time we give the younger crowd the opportunity to move the company forward. I will be 66 years old in June, and there are things I want to accomplish in life before I am too old. The land refinancing will be complete before June, and the most logical date for me to step aside is the first of July, which would be the start of a new fiscal year."

Hoke responded, "I think that timetable is generous and appreciate your willingness to stay through the transition. You went to Investa because Morgan Stanley asked you to, but you stayed because of an obligation to the employees. You should be proud of what you and the team have accomplished."

We talked about a succession plan; we did not feel any individual at Investa at that time had both the experience and skill set to lead the entire company, but there were several employees fully capable of running divisions. With what the company had been through, I was reluctant to bring in an outsider and advocated we split the company into at least two divisions with a CEO for each division.

At subsequent board meetings in the following months, we discussed my succession at length. I proposed that Campbell Hanan run the office company, and Cameron Holt run the land company. We would have a small residual corporate staff for financial reporting across both companies.

The board agreed to try the dual approach beginning the first of March 2013, but reserved the right to change the structure. I planned to be in residence at least until July 1, so we had four months to trial the approach. Unfortunately, it did not go exactly as planned; nothing at Investa ever seemed to go as anticipated.

At the same time, our land loan, which had been refinanced in 2009 and 2011, was maturing again in June and was facing some resistance from the lender, ANZ Bank. The bankers were not happy that Ming was to be part of the office group and would not be accountable for land company operations. Ming, Jonathan, and I were the face of Investa to the banks, and I was retiring and Ming and

Jonathan were going to the office group. They put the land refinance on hold.

One evening, I met Nigel Williams, head of risk for ANZ, at a cocktail party sponsored by the Art Gallery of New South Wales. Nigel and I were on the Presidents Committee of the gallery and were friendly. Nigel asked if Ming would still be responsible for a refinanced land loan and seemed uncomfortable with my response. Later, Eddie Law and James Amarti of ANZ met with me privately and told me that without Ming being responsible, the bank would not proceed with the land refinance. No other bank had indicated any interest in financing our land portfolio; we were in a difficult position. I promised Eddie and James that Ming would have responsibility for the land loan, and I would make sure this was clear in any subsequent Investa organizational structure. With that promise, the bank re-engaged on the land refinance.

Shortly thereafter, I met with Campbell and told him that Ming and Jonathan would have dual reporting responsibilities because of the need to keep both of them involved in corporate-wide activities, including the land financing. He felt it would confuse internal staff and outsiders if he were not clearly designated as Ming's and Jonathan's boss.

I was not concerned; I hoped to sell the management company to our listed fund, Investa Office fund (IOF), and internalize IOF's management. The timing seemed good to me; investors wanted an internally managed IOF, and IOF could afford to pay a high price for our office management company. I was unhappy dealing with succession and related management issues; they would become the responsibility of the IOF's capable independent board of directors including Debbie Page, Peter Rowe, and Peter Dodd.

In early May 2013, I flew to New York City to discuss succession with senior executives of MSREF. We discussed internalization of IOF for a couple of hours, but there were too many issues that needed to be resolved before everyone felt comfortable with triggering a near-term internalization. My pending departure and concerns about company performance under new leadership, the uncertainty of Morgan Stanley's exit strategy and timing, and an increasingly challenging economy were some of the factors considered. We all believed that internalization of Investa into IOF would be a good outcome

In the days that followed, Hoke, Chris Tynan, and I talked frequently about succession. We wanted a plan for me to take back to Sydney. The employees and Investa executives were expecting a decision.

We finally agreed to leave Ming and Jonathan in the corporate group and continue their corporate-wide responsibilities for finance, legal, reporting, and corporate transactions. Then everyone in office would report to Campbell, and our bankers would be happy and move forward to refinance the land business. I flew back to Sydney believing we had solved the succession problem.

That Friday at our group executive meeting, I explained the revised plan. Some of the executives did not respond well. The company had split into factions after my pending departure had become clear. What had been a cohesive and mutually supportive team began to break down.

I should not have been surprised. It is not uncommon for corporate executives to compete for position when a dominant leader steps down and succession is imminent.

I met with each executive individually. A couple days later, the executive team met. I declined to attend as did Cameron Holt, who was working diligently with his Land team and staying far away from the internal debate that was consuming the office group executives. The group executives decided to work together in the shared organizational structure and move past the recent differences that had surfaced.

The board of directors met in late May, and we debated how best to proceed. With some reluctance and concern, we agreed to move forward with the plan that Hoke, Chris, and I had originally formulated. I promised to be available on short notice to return to Investa and take charge if things melted down again.

Subsequently, Ming was offered a job as CFO of a large REIT in Sydney, which caused great concern. After considerable discussion, Ming decided to stay at Investa, to our collective relief. She told me of her decision one Monday morning at 8 a.m. over coffee.

Later that day I encountered James Amati at lunch; he told me the ANZ bank land refinancing should be documented within a couple of weeks. I did not mention we almost had another detour.

The next day, my assistant Elpie hosted a birthday party for me at Investa. I used the excuse of getting all the employees together to announce my retirement as CEO of Investa Property Trust. After five years of rolling from crisis to crisis and solution to solution, it was time for me to step back. I wanted to tell the employees of my plans first; then we issued a press release celebrating the future of Investa. I remained chairman of the Investa boards.

Reflecting on my career and the Investa experience, I have always felt a keen responsibility to the investors who put up the money to fund the companies I work for with the expectation of a reasonable return on their investment. Often the investors are pension funds, which represent the future retirement of workers, who have spent their lives working in expectation of retiring someday with sufficient proceeds to pay for their needs. Many of the investors in Investa are pension funds, and I felt the responsibility to return as much of their investment as I can. I clearly felt responsible to the Morgan Stanley team as well.

I also felt a great responsibility to repay any loans that we borrowed from lenders. The story of Investa is filled with lending issues, and in the darkest economic times, the banks supported Investa. I cannot imagine not repaying their loans with interest per the terms of each and every loan document. When Investa borrowed money, I felt as if I personally were incurring the debt. My colleagues felt the same way.

Balancing my sense of obligation to our investors and lenders, I also felt responsible to ensure that our employees are fairly treated. They deserved a supportive and professional work environment, and if the company is successful, part of that success should be shared with the employees who contributed to the outcome.

Finally, every company owes a responsibility to the community in which it operates. We all should strive to leave the world a better place, and there is no better place to start than in the community, which provides us services and shelter. Investa has been a corporate leader in Australia, supporting the communities in which we work and taking a leadership role in environmental sustainability.

Investa continued under the very capable leadership of Jonathan Callaghan, Michael Cook, Campbell Hanan, Cameron Holt, Ming Long, Pete Menegazzo, and many others. Toby Phelps (IOF Fund Manager) subsequently resigned to move back to London, after providing much appreciated leadership for IOF and its investors. Ming Long was appointed as his replacement as fund manager after the land loan was refinanced. Jonathan Callaghan became managing director of all the Investa companies and quickly earned the respect and support of the Investa employees and the investors. Since my departure as CEO, the companies which constitute Investa have performed at an exemplary level.

TWENTY-FIVE KEY LESSONS FROM THE OFFICE

I have had a terrific career. I was asked recently to give advice to a young colleague based on my experience. In this chapter, I have attempted to answer her request.

It seems that there is no end of books promising success and riches by adopting one scheme or another. In real estate, the get-rich schemes usually involve borrowing more money than is reasonable or prudent, and planning to never experience any setbacks or problems. My experience is that there is no substitute for a commitment to hard work, careful planning, and good organization. Let me share the twenty-five most important lessons I have learned in my career.

1. **Don't expect anyone to give you anything.**

I cannot remember a period of time when I did not work. After my father died, I had specific chores at home. In grade school and junior high school, I did yard work for neighbors, had a paper route, and washed dishes at my junior high. In high school, I bagged groceries, stocked shelves in a neighborhood pharmacy, and worked in a fiberglass factory. A key lesson from decades of work is as follows: If you need or want something, work for it. You will appreciate it more and not be indebted to anyone.

2. **You make your own luck.**

Nothing in my life that I can think of has been the result of luck.

A former football coach at the University of Texas used to say, "Luck is the result when preparation meets opportunity." I can't improve on that saying.

3. Being successful is more than just working hard. It is being organized, planning, and working smart as well as working hard. It is choosing to focus effort where there is reward.

When I was in elementary school, I recall singing a song with my friend, John Kilborne, in front of the class, as part of some requirement. One verse went "19 tons and what do you get, another day older and deeper in debt." The song was about coal miners who worked hard but never made enough money to pay their bills.

I have met many people in my life that worked hard but never made much money or achieved satisfactory career objectives. Working hard is only part of the equation for success.

4. Losers have the best excuses.

Winners find a way to succeed despite the roadblocks and unexpected difficulties. People who are unsuccessful often reach for excuses. When you hear someone making an excuse, you are probably dealing with a loser.

Whenever things go wrong, and things always go wrong at some point, look in the mirror for answers. When unforeseen challenges arise or setbacks are encountered, too often those affected look to blame others or circumstances beyond their influence.

Successful people focus on what they can do to respond to setbacks and do not waste time playing a blame game or feeling sorry for themselves. Blame does not solve problems and neither do excuses.

5. It is important to pick a job not based on immediate compensation but on how it prepares you to realize future opportunities.

My first job after graduate school was with Gladstone Associates in Washington, D.C. Gladstone was a prestigious management consulting firm specializing in real estate. I was fortunate to get a job there and, in fact, turned down other, initially more lucrative jobs for the opportunity to work at Gladstone. Like all top quality professional service firms, the hours were very long but the breadth of learning was incredible. Typically, I worked twelve- to fourteen-hour days, six days a week, and juggled five to ten assignments concurrently. I learned more about real estate in five years at Gladstone than I could have learned in more than ten years elsewhere.

I have always learned of jobs through personal contacts, which I believe is typical. I have been offered jobs based on favorable impressions of people familiar with my work. I have never had a job offer based on submission of a resume or request for an interview.

As a corporate CEO, I have received many resumes, probably thousands during my career. I do not recall ever hiring someone because of an unsolicited resume I received. Sending out resumes is generally useless, in my experience, unless it is for a first job that requires no experience.

6.   If you know a firm will not ultimately succeed, don't hang around and wait for someone else to turn off the lights.

After a few months working with a company in Philadelphia, problems were very apparent. The company reported favorable earnings each quarter but had developed very little real estate despite incurring large expenses. Beware of firms who use accounting trickery to enhance results, even if the accountants assure such practices are legal and common. In my view, the company used accounting techniques to make results look better than they were.

I resigned after only one year. I was unsure where to go when I realized this company would not be successful, but I did not want to waste more time there. A few years later, the company was closed and the assets sold to a competitor, but I had already moved on.

A friend from graduate school, John Slidell, lived and worked in Annapolis, and told me his firm's workload required hiring another senior employee. Soon after, I joined John and moved to Annapolis. There is always another job waiting for someone willing to work hard.

7.   Never stay where you are uncomfortable ethically.

Despite interesting work negotiating joint ventures between cities and private developers, and creating and implementing urban redevelopment projects, I do not have favorable memories of working at the Maryland consulting firm. One of the partners often sold services to communities in need of help and then did as little work as possible to maximize company profit. In one case, I put together a consortium of professional firms and bid successfully on a large contract. After we were notified our bid was successful, the partner intervened and made it clear we were keeping most of the money and not doing much of the work as a reward for winning this bid. I was disgusted and quit.

There is no acceptable reason to remain with an ethically challenged employer. There are better career opportunities elsewhere, and you will feel better working somewhere that values ethics and moral behavior.

8.   No matter how important the project, life is too short to have to deal with assholes.

I had a "no asshole" rule at Center America and subsequent companies. If someone cannot deal with you professionally and ethically, just pass on the deal and move on. There will be other deals. I may have lost an occasional deal but overall my companies enjoyed good success and reputation, which led to other and better opportunities.

9.   Players score points but teams win games.

To be successful, any organization must have a culture of teamwork. Individual stars must be supportive of the team concept, or those individuals should be moved on. I once fired a top chief financial officer who was good at his job, but thought it unnecessary to work with colleagues and was dismissive of others' ideas. The entire company performed better after his departure.

10. After you make the sale, get out of the house.

Years ago I met a fellow who sold vacuum cleaners door to door. When I asked what made him successful, he told me after he made the sale, he exited as quickly as possible before the buyer developed remorse. Too many people in business and life do not know when to close the deal and move on.

11. Always leave a few nickels on the table.

Ernie Hahn once told me never to negotiate a deal that was so onerous that your opponent is left with nothing but hard feelings. Leave a few nickels on the table that you could have taken. That way your opponent will bring you the next deal or at least recommend you to others.

12. Procrastinators usually come in last place.

There are so many unanticipated challenges that occur in almost every decision process, and those who do not finish the known and anticipated tasks early often lack sufficient time to react fully to these last-minute and unanticipated events. In business and in life, people who procrastinate ultimately fall behind those who are better organized and finish tasks early.

13. Be a wall pusher.

Early in my career I met a successful businessman in Oklahoma. I asked him what he did to be so successful. He said he was a "wall pusher." When you move forward in life and in business, there are always walls in the way, preventing progress. When you try to push the obstructing walls away, someone on the other side always pushes back. You need patience and perseverance to keep pushing; eventually the other guy will tire and move away.

14. Be a good listener.

You never learn anything when you are talking. You only learn when others talk and you listen. Sometimes I tell my staff when we are about to go into an important meeting, "Please resist the temptation to talk."

Being a good listener is an art. Understanding what the key issues and priorities are of those you are meeting with should lead to better agreements and outcomes.

15.   It is important to recognize change and get ahead of the change curve. Too many are focused on the rearview mirror rather than the road ahead.

The status quo develops its own constituency who benefit from keeping things the way they are. Yet, successful people find a way to implement change. I have been told "you cannot do that" hundreds of times, but when change is the correct path, I generally find a way to go there. Successful people do not merely follow the path of others; they lead, often in new and challenging directions.

It is also important to recognize changing conditions and make personal adjustments in anticipation of such changes. I joined Barton-Aschman Associates, a consulting firm, in 1978. Much of my work there was providing financial and market-research services to shopping center developers. However, in the early 1980s, major shopping mall developers began to hire market and financial staff rather than rely on consultants, and I realized my primary – although not exclusive – practice area would become a declining business for consultants. When the Hahn Company called and offered me a job to organize their market and financial research, I accepted, although it meant moving the family from Evanston, which we loved, to distant San Diego.

A couple of years after I resigned from Barton-Aschman, a larger engineering firm from California acquired the firm. My former research group was terminated. If I had remained in Evanston, I would most likely have been unemployed at a time when our family needs were great.

16.   In competitive markets, decision-making should be localized. Corporate bureaucracy smothers innovation, slows speed to market, and ultimately leads to failure.

The corporate bureaucracy associated with my tenure at W.R.

Grace Properties meant real estate decisions were made too slowly, giving advantage to local, more nimble competitors. This inability to react quickly and the reliance on accounting tricks led to the demise of the Grace subsidiary in my judgment.

At Plaza Properties, Center America, and New Plan, I instituted localized decision-making, which resulted in significant increases in performance. Generally, locally based staffs are better positioned to make correct local decisions than faraway corporate executives or centralized organization bosses. Good financial controls and excellent communication technology are keys to decentralized decision models.

17.   Whenever you are invited to perform on a bigger stage, it is critical to take full advantage and demonstrate the capability to move on to bigger and more significant tasks.

Soon after joining the Hahn Company, I received a call from Trizec's CEO (Trizec Corporation owned Hahn) and was asked to undertake detailed financial analyses of all our properties in a very short timeframe, despite limited hardware, software, and support people. No one at Hahn thought it was possible to accomplish the task within the allowed timetable. The Trizec CEO was known to be a very tough taskmaster and almost impossible to satisfy.

Exceeding expectations was the key, which is often the case. My staff, including Bill Speer, and I worked round the clock for three months and turned out detailed financial reports on every mall (about 45) we owned including graphs, charts, and cash flows. Harold Milavsky, Trizec's CEO, and Kevin Benson, the president of Trizec, flew down for the presentation and were impressed, and my position within the firm was greatly enhanced.

18.   One important key to personal business success is to develop an expertise in something that adds value and others do not have.

I became the expert at Hahn in market research – including being able to predict the sales of future shopping centers to be developed, based on local demographic models we developed with the help of a statistician. With new personal computers and advanced budgeting models, I could also determine the likely financial impact of proposed property investments. The company did not make an investment decision without consulting me.

With a unique expertise, I was able to branch out and take on related responsibilities. Soon I was in charge of all new investments for Hahn including acquisitions and new development. As head of new business, I was involved in key corporate executive discussions.

19. Not everything in business is fair.

After turning around Plaza Properties of America and then transforming the Hahn Company as acting CEO, I expected to be promoted to CEO of Hahn. However, the Hahn Company's corporate owner, Trizec, was acquired by another company during this time. A new Trizec board member, Jerry O'Connor, recommended a friend of his to be CEO of Hahn. Most of the new board did not know me and followed Jerry's recommendation. I resigned as COO a couple months later. I believed the decision was unfair to me, and a shock to staff and industry colleagues, but I needed to move on and focus on the future.

Chris Niehaus of Morgan Stanley called and offered me the job of CEO of a company Morgan Stanley had acquired in Houston, Texas. It was another corporate turnaround assignment, and I accepted the offer and became CEO of Center America Property Trust in 1995.

After my departure, the Hahn Company (then called Trizec Hahn Centers) lost about $1 billion in poorly conceived and executed projects, and the Hahn Company's assets were sold and the company was closed.

20. To achieve success, sacrifice is often required, and the family bears the greatest burden.

After I was passed over for the Hahn CEO position, I could not stay there and work for the new CEO. My wife understood this, although the move from San Diego was a major sacrifice for her and my sons, Andrew and Ross. Jill was president of the local school board, Andrew was about to enter high school, and Ross's best friend and cousin lived a block away. No one wanted to move to Houston, but the family supported me.

We did achieve success at Center America and the family adjusted well to life in Houston. If I had stayed at Hahn and in San Diego, I almost certainly would have found myself unemployed with considerable expenses and limited prospects when the company closed a few years later.

21.   It is easier to achieve great success when starting from a low level of performance, and opportunities are generally more available in underperforming and poorly performing companies. In such situations, however, it is important to negotiate a favorable contract to insure you participate fully in the upside if you do achieve success.

Most people want to work for a successful company, but opportunities may actually be better elsewhere. When I took the reins of Center America in 1995, the company was losing money at a rapid rate, and the properties were worse than I had imagined. If I had not had family responsibilities then, I probably would have quit six months after starting. Things were bleak.

Eventually, with lots of hard work, long hours, and Morgan Stanley capital, the corporate ship began to turn. I replaced most of the staff in the first year, set up new systems and programs, relocated the firm to new office space, and created a professional work environment.

Gradually, the company began to generate positive cash flow. I also negotiated a very favorable employment agreement for myself and favorable financial incentive programs for key staff.

In late 2001, we agreed to sell Center America to New Plan Excel Realty Trust and that made all of the hard work and late night worries at Center America worthwhile. Financially, my family was more secure than it had ever been. The transaction was a win for the investors, the seller, the buyer, Center America employees, and for the MacDonald family.

22. In everyone's life I believe there is presented an opportunity to hit a home run and win the game, but you have to swing the bat. Prior to that at-bat, there are years of preparation. When the time arises, however, it is important to step up and take advantage of the opportunity.

I have had several good swings in my career. Taking on the "bad bank," Plaza Properties of America, was a big risk but worked out well. Most of my colleagues at the time thought I was nuts leaving the security of the big Hahn mother ship for the risk of a lesser undercapitalized portfolio of second-tier properties.

Center America was a "home run" outcome although it also entailed considerable risk, including moving my family to faraway Houston and taking responsibility for a portfolio of largely dilapidated properties. Investa was also a successful outcome despite the considerable odds. When offered an opportunity to score the winning run, understand the situation and risks involved, but also recognize that if you never step up to the plate you will never hit the long ball.

23. Maintain your health regardless of pressures at work and in life.

Beware of stress. I once watched a woman in the kitchen of a fast food chain restaurant. She rushed from microwave to broiler to grill with such fury, trying to keep up with the flow of orders at a busy lunchtime. That is a stressful job. Everyone has stress in their job, and I have certainly had my share. But some people deal with stress better than others, and the consequences of not dealing with stress can be deadly.

I have the genes of my father, who died at age 47. I am still alive at 68 due in part to successfully managing stress. For years I ran distances regularly, and now I use other aerobic exercises to avoid my father's fate. Exercise is a great stress manager. No matter how busy you are, find time to exercise regularly. Your life depends on it.

24. Family is first.

I have travelled millions of miles during my career and met thousands of successful people. When I talk with older, successful people, they often comment that they wished they had spent more time with their families during their careers. I have never met anyone who complained he or she spent too much time with his or her family. The competitive work environment places huge pressures on our time and energy, but work is just the means to care for your family and that priority should not be forgotten.

The old adage, "Blood is thicker than water," is true. Take care of your family and expect them to take care of you.

25. Despite my age and long career span, I find opportunities to learn something new almost every day. Whenever you become satisfied with what you already know, your pace will slow, and you will soon be passed by those who continue to learn and adjust to ever-changing markets and conditions.

The fast-paced environment in which we live presents unusual and significant challenges. In business and life, experience is valuable in confronting issues, especially ones similar to those previously encountered. As we age, we accumulate greater experience and typically can contribute greater value.

What is distinctly different today, however, are the issues that we confront may well be very different from the issues we experienced previously. The tools we used to solve past problems, especially technology-aided tools, may be very different than the ones we need to solve current problems. Experience per se provides less value than in the past.

We cannot rely on experience to the extent past generations may have been able to. We need to stay current, we need to keep learning, and we need to keep expanding our experiences. We must constantly adjust, which is not a comfortable or secure position. But we have no choice except to watch others pass us by.

EPILOGUE

Much has happened since I wrote this book. Personally, my sister, Judy, and my brother, Bing, both died suddenly and unexpectedly. I miss them both terribly. Their passing and the birth of my granddaughter, Claire, reinforce our transitory existence and the need to live our brief lives fully and productively.

I have always wanted to leave the world a bit better off when I depart, and I hope my life has benefitted others who I have shared it with. I am immensely proud of my sons, Andrew and Ross, and believe they will both contribute to a better place. My mission going forward is to establish community scholarships, which make funds available for those financially unable to attend university without incurring so much debt. In return, I expect recipients of my scholarships and fellowships to help others in need. My plan to help others is more fully explained at the website macdonaldscholars.com. Davidson College, the University of North Carolina, and Indiana University have adopted this pay-it-forward scholarship program, and I am in discussions with other universities.

Morgan Stanley sold the various parts of Investa in 2015 and 2016. Actually, they sold three companies in three separate transactions. Investa Land was sold to Proprium, a U.S.-based investment company. The principals at Proprium were very familiar with the track record and quality of the land platform and its management. They offered the highest bid. All of the Investa Land employees were retained, and the company is planning a major expansion of operations in Australia.

CIC, the Chinese Investment Corporation, which is a sovereign wealth fund, purchased the office building assets in what we formerly called the Hold portfolio. They outbid several other global and Australian investors, and offered a record-setting price for Investa's high quality portfolio. The Investa employees responsible for managing the assets moved from Investa to Mirvac, which negotiated the management contract with CIC. Campbell Hanan also moved to Mirvac, assuming responsibility for all of Mirvac's office and industrial portfolios. Mirvac paid the Morgan Stanley partnership for the portfolio management contract.

The office management company was purchased by the Investa Commercial Property Fund (ICPF). ICPF was the small institutional fund on which we focused all of our attention after selling or closing the remainder of our funds business. At the time of purchase, ICPF had grown to about $3 billion in assets under the leadership of Pete Menegazzo. The independent ICPF board directors, led by David Baffsky, initiated and then negotiated the deal, which was approved by a unanimous vote of the investors in the fund. The plan is to retain virtually all of the Investa employees and expand the fund through future acquisitions.

IOF's independent directors and the fund manager, Ming Long, working on behalf of the directors, sought to break from ICPF and common ownership of the two funds, and solicited bids from outside investors, to the potential detriment of the Morgan Stanley partnership's investment and many of the Investa employees. They were able to solicit a mostly non-cash bid from Dexus, another listed Australian REIT. Dexus indicated they were not interested in accepting Investa employees but would allow such employees to apply for jobs as desired. The amount of money lost if IOF sold to Dexus or another buyer was relatively negligible in the scope of the overall deal, but the terrific and hard-working Investa team would have been broken up if the Dexus bid was successful.

Leading up to the unit holder vote in early April 2016, the debate was vigorous and, at times, acrimonious. Those in favor of the Dexus bid tried to block Morgan Stanley from voting its units, but the Australian Supreme Court affirmed Morgan Stanley's right to vote. Supporters of the sale accused Morgan Stanley of being conflicted and advocating their own interests. From my perspective, such accusations were unfair and inaccurate. I believe Morgan Stanley was acting in the best interests of their investors and IOF investors. Morgan Stanley executives thought the Dexus proposal did not reflect fair value based on their experience. We talked more about the employees' welfare and preserving the high-performance Investa platform than about any financial benefits to Morgan Stanley.

IOF's independent directors also felt unfairly accused of refusing an earlier Morgan Stanley offer and advocating a less-desired deal. I believe they felt their ability to work in the best interest of the IOF unit holders was being undermined by a variety of forces including unfavorable media coverage.

Reportedly, the IOF independent directors had agreed to pay their advisors a bonus of $18 million if the Dexus proposal (or a similar proposal) were approved and very little if the bid failed. This financial motivation for the advisors contributed to the acrimony in my judgment.

On April 15, 2016, the Dexus proposal was voted down by the IOF unit holders. The next week, the fund manager and the IOF independent directors resigned. The future of IOF will be subsequently determined similar to any listed company. I personally hope the Investa platform will remain together and continue to provide IOF investors with superior results.

After paying all of their outstanding debt, Morgan Stanley's investors recovered most of their original investment. Had we been forced into insolvency during our crises, investors would have received nothing. Had we defaulted on loans, major banks would have incurred significant losses. By my calculation the investors lost considerably less of their investments than comparable companies in Australia during the same timeframe.

Investa was acquired in 2007 by Morgan Stanley's private equity real estate fund, which utilized high levels of debt and comparatively small amounts of equity to complete the transaction. This was a typical strategy with private equity and hedge funds in 2007. By using mostly debt, returns on equity can be very high when the market moves favorably. However, when the market moves down, the result is often bankruptcy and job loss. Many iconic companies were badly damaged by such strategies including the *Chicago Tribune* and *Los Angeles Times*, Chrysler, and retailers like Linens 'n Things.

The use of debt is encouraged by public tax policy. Interest on debt is tax deductible; the taxpayer is subsidizing these high-risk investments, which often result in job loss and corporate destruction. Unlike debt, dividends or equity distributions are taxed. The logical way to discourage over-leveraged, debt-driven investment strategies is to make the interest on debt non-deductible on taxes, or at least make interest above a certain threshold – like 50 percent of value – non-deductible. Until the excessive use of debt is no longer subsidized, there will continue to be debt-fueled corporate takeovers and bankruptcies. Hard-working people will lose jobs that otherwise would have been preserved, and local communities will lose key employers and related taxes unnecessarily.

Morgan Stanley made a badly timed investment in 2007. But when the severity of the problem became clear, they supported Investa with equity and expertise. Chris Niehaus, Steve Harker, Hoke Slaughter, Chris Tynan, and Peter Harned and their colleagues were always available to discuss difficult situations, regardless of the time of day or day of week. The Morgan Stanley team deserves credit for staying the course and supporting the company even in the darkest of times.

I was subsequently contacted about taking on another corporate CEO turnaround assignment but declined. Been there and done that, and now I have other priorities including establishing programs at universities to support students financially, and enable them to help others in need. I still have so much to accomplish.

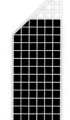

ACKNOWLEDGMENTS

I have had the privilege of working with many talented and supportive colleagues during my career. There are far too many to list, but a few that come to mind, and who made a significant contribution to the corporate successes I have been involved with, include the following. Each person is only listed once even if he or she worked at multiple companies. I am forever in their debt.

Plaza Properties of America
Donna Balderama, Greg Beyer, Marilyn and Danielle Bochstahler, Steve Bowers, Bob Doherty, Rick Froese, Mike Heiken, Dave Hirsch

The Hahn Company
Cheryl Berkey, Al Corti, Alberta Davidson, Bill Doyle, Wayne Findley, John Gilchrist, Teri Powers, Vernon Schwartz, Bill Speer, Bob Sorenson

Center America
Mike Axelrad, Charley Carver, Gary Cunningham, John Gilluly, Lamar Haggard, Glen Havens, Linda McGee, Dan Muniza, Robert Scott, Tex Speer, Mike Tones

New Plan Excel
Dean Bernstein, Rick Brenner, Len Brumberg, Mike Carroll, Carolyn Carter, Stacy Lipschitz, Tom Litzler, John Roche, Glenn Rufrano, Steve Siegel, John Waters, Mark Worley

Morgan Stanley Real Estate Funds

Glenn Aaronson, John Buza, Mike Foster, Willem de Geus, Peter Harned, Sonny Kalsi, John Klopp, Michael Levy, Jay Mantz, Hugh Macdonnell, Tim Morris, Chris Niehaus, Brian Niles, Olivier du Poulpiquet, Hoke Slaughter, Owen Thomas, Chris Tynan

Investa

Elizabeth Brearley, Jonathan Callaghan, Michael Chan, Michael Cook, Bonita Croft, Beck Dawson, Paul Fletcher, Sally Franklin, Ivan Gorridge, Campbell Hanan, Bruce Harper, Cameron Holt, Nathan Huon, Lloyd Jenkins, Greg Kerr, Jeff King, Emily Lee-Waldo, Jason Leong, Ming Long, Pete Menegazzo, Andrew Murray, Neal Noble, Paul O'Brien, Collette O'Reilly, Christine O'Hara, Roger Parker, Duncan Peacock, Toby Phelps, Janice Punch, Craig Roussiac, Michael Royle, Ian Schilling, David Stabback, Mark Tait, Tina Tang, Elpie Vanos, Glen Watts

Investa Partners and Friends

James Armati, David Baffsky, Peter Barnes, Andrew Balzan, Paul Bartlett, Mark Coleman, Julia Diem, Peter Dodd, Shayne Elliott, Jim Evans, George Giovas, Steve Harker, Narelle Hooper, Peter King, Eddie Law, Mark Lloyd, Erryn Lloyd-Jones, Michael Madunic, Gail McKenzie, Mark Monaghan, Garry Moody, Gary Newman, Debbie Page, Spiro Pappas, Peter Rowe, Lynn Thurber, Dennis Wildenburg, Rob Whitfield

Other Colleagues

David Perisho, Gene Pinover, Mike Pruter

Supportive Family and a Special Person

Judy Anderson, Bing and Molly MacDonald, Margot and Norm Welch, Patti Kurtz

Profits from the sale of this book will go to support need-based college scholarships.

For more information on MacDonald Community Scholarships, please visit: macdonaldscholars.com